Rethinking Social De

Socialist History 27

Rivers Oram Press
London, Sydney and Chicago

Editorial Enquiries: Kevin Morgan, School of Social Sciences, University of Manchester, Manchester M13 9PL or kevin.morgan@manchester.ac.uk.

Reviews Enquiries: John Callaghan, School of Humanities, Languages and Social Sciences, University of Wolverhampton, Wulfruna Street, Wolverhampton WV1 1PB or j.callaghan@wlv.ac.uk

Socialist History 27 was edited by Kevin Morgan, John Callaghan and Willie Thompson

Published in 2005
by Rivers Oram Press, an imprint of Rivers Oram Publishers Ltd
144 Hemingford Road, London, N1 1DE

Distributed in the USA by
Independent Publishers Group, Franklin Street, Chicago, IL 60610
Distributed in Australia and New Zealand by
UNIReps, University of New South Wales, Sydney, NSW 2052

Set in Garamond by NJ Design
and printed in Great Britain by T.J. International Ltd, Padstow

British Library Cataloguing in Publication Data
A catalogue record for this publication is available from the British Library
ISBN 1 85489 160 X (pb)
ISSN 0969 4331

Contents

Jean-François Fayet, *Karl Radek (1885-1939): Biographie politique* (Brian Pearce)

Charles Ashleigh, *The Rambling Kid: A Novel about the IWW* (David Howell)

Francis Wheen, *How Mumbo-Jumbo Conquered the World: A Short History of Modern Delusions* (Willie Thompson)

Beverly J. Silver, *Forces of Labor. Workers' Movements and Globalization since 1870* (Steve Ludlam)

Martin van Gelderen and Quentin Skinner (eds), *Republicanism. A Shared European Heritage* (Steven Fielding)

Steven Fielding, *The Labour Governments 1964–1970,* vol.1: *Labour and Cultural Change* (Julia Speht)

John Keane, *Global Civil Society?* (Alan Apperley)

Lawrence Black, *The Political Culture of the Left in Affluent Britain, 1951–64. Old Labour, New Britain?* (Jeremy Nuttall)

Catherine Epstein, *The Last Revolutionaries: German Communists and Their Century* (Stephen Hopkins)

Matthew Worley (ed.), *In Search of Revolution: International Communist Parties in the Third Period* (Jean-François Fayet)

Notes on Contributors

Stefan Berger is a member of the *Socialist History* editorial board and has written extensively on European social democracy and comparative labour history. He is professor of modern and contemporary history at the University of Glamorgan.

Mark Bevir is associate professor of political science at UC Berkeley. He is the author of *The Logic of the History of Ideas* (1999), co-author of *Interpreting British Governance* (2003), and coeditor of *Critiques of Capital: Transatlantic Exchanges 1800 to the Present Day* (2003).

Aad Blok is managing editor and book review editor of the *International Review of Social History* at the International Institute of Social History, Amsterdam. He has co-edited volumes on social democracy and the agrarian issue 1870–1914, and on the role of labour in information revolutions.

Donald Sassoon is professor of comparative European history at Queen Mary, University of London. His much-acclaimed *One Hundred Years of Socialism: the West European left in the twentieth century* was published in 1996. He is an editorial adviser to *Socialist History*.

Andrew Thorpe is professor of history at the University of Exeter. His recent publications include *The British Communist Party and Moscow* (2000) and *A History of the British Labour Party* (second edn, 2001).

Robert Taylor is policy adviser to the European Trade Union Confederation in Brussels. Former labour editor of the *Observer* and then the *Financial Times*, he is writing a history of the parliamentary Labour Party since 1906.

Willie Thompson is a former editor of *Socialist History* and a member of its editorial board.

Editorial

As indicated in our last issue, *Socialist History* is one of the sponsors of a series of three major conferences on the theme *Rethinking Social Democracy*. The first of these, held in London in April 2004, dealt specifically with historical perspectives on social democracy and a sample of the papers presented, along with commentaries and an interview developing issues raised at the conference, provide the main contents of our present issue.

Specifically, the conference title indicated a concern with the interaction of social-democratic politics with issues of culture and society. Many papers focused explicitly on this interaction, but the three days of the conference also underlined how any political movement of this scope has to be understood in terms of a number of contexts and relationships. One, brought out strongly in the international character of the conference itself, is that of sister movements and parties in different countries, which in a few papers were discussed in an explicitly comparative context. Another, shaping these movements in rather different ways, were the forms of competition and interaction with other political movements and intellectual traditions. A third, the particular focus of the first conference, was the development of social democracy over the course of the twentieth century, leading to the challenges that currently confront all sections of the left at the beginning of the present one. It was in an appreciation of the scale of these challenges that the origins of these conferences lay, as a contribution to a much wider discussion.

As a historian of social democracy whose work stands out for its comparative scope and insight, Stefan Berger is well placed to take account of these different dimensions of the subject. In his article, 'Communism, social democracy and the democracy gap', he not only addresses the dichotomy between these rival political movements of the left, but suggests that underlying this dichotomy was a shared tendency to neglect or depreciate issues of democracy as opposed to social and economic reform. Of course, there is no suggested conflation of the two movements: as Berger indicates, there was a world of difference between neglect and active denial or suppression. Nevertheless, the 'democracy gap' which he identifies suggests both challenges and opportunities now that dichotomy has given way to fragmentation and lack of momentum. At the same time, perhaps the sensitivities of the left to issues of power and subjection in spheres beyond the customary limits of 'democracy', for example in the world of work, may help identify gaps within democracy itself, at least as conventionally practised.

Andrew Thorpe's article also addresses an issue of wide significance in twentieth-century politics: the relationship between social democracy and liberalism. Specifically he examines the relationship between the Labour and Liberal parties in Britain between the wars and suggests that retrospective counterfactuals as to a possible broad centre-left ignore a host of deep-seated tensions, from leadership and organisation to ideology and ethos. Especially salutary is his reminder, as against the countless advocacies of a progressive alliance of a popular front, that neither the Liberal Party nor its supporters can automatically be identified with its more radical leadership figures and their programmes. Perhaps there is another issue of how far Liberal ideas, electors and even candidates found their way into the new progressive narrative of Labour's forward march, as it supplanted the Liberals organisationally. To the extent that it did so, perhaps we should be looking, not for the old Gladstonian radical agendas, but for the reforming, top-down, state-collectivist Liberalism of the Edwardian years. That is something that is also missing from romantic Liberal counterfactuals. Perhaps it was not the disappearance of Liberalism but its very tenacity, in the too-easily forgotten tradition of Belloc's Servile State, that made its own contribution to Labour's own democracy gap.

Aad Blok's discussion of the Dutch social-democratic economist, Jan Tinbergen, suggests the possibility of further hidden connections. Tinbergen, Blok suggests, might be regarded as the very type of the 'expert-intellectual', whose principal agency of reform was the state and whose measure of economic order was efficiency. In this, Tinbergen bears a marked family resemblance to those Edwardian Fabian experts, who after permeating the Liberal-Conservative establishment, turned to permeating the Labour Party— to such effect as to draft its founding programme. What they lacked, and Tinbergen's generation developed, was the key to an effective reformist economic strategy, rooted in Planism and Keynesian insights, while, in Tinbergen's case, increasingly accepting the postulates of a system of free enterprise. Conceived as a sort of 'third way', beyond the traditional dichotomy of left and right, Blok shows how in Cold War Europe Tinbergen was moved not least by considerations of individual liberty. At the same time, the determining functions of the social engineer within Tinbergen's mixed economy once again raise the spectre of the democracy gap. Intriguingly, the comparison is suggested with Hugh Dalton: a quintessential Labour politician, but one rooted in Edwardian Fabianism and (according to Beatrice Webb) initially forsaking Liberalism for Labour on grounds of his career.

One of the keynote speakers at the first RSD conference was Donald Sassoon, who offered his broader reflections on the social-democratic contribution to social and political reform over the course of the twentieth century. Many of his arguments will, of course, be familiar to readers through his seminal *One Hundred Years of Socialism*. Here, in an interview with Willie Thompson, Sassoon situates his understanding of social democracy in his own practice as a historian 'without manifestoes'. Here perhaps there is a tension between intention, articulation and political consequences which casts a further light on the democracy gap. Perhaps it is true, as Sassoon suggests, that any left or centre-left party of government has to accept the constraints of an integrated capitalist system. And yet, as he also points out, the reforms of capitalism itself were also the unintended results of a fear of the left—a sentiment and an incentive to reform which it is hard to imagine being brought about by parties circumscribed even in opposition by the anticipated constraints of office. At least it is conceivable that effective pressures for reform do not always take the form of reformism. And if that is so, perhaps there is a further paradox: that often it was movements whose formal commitment to democracy was weak or fatally compromised, which nevertheless functioned as democratising forces to the extent that they challenged existing structures and dispositions of power. In part this may register the paradox of communist parties demanding democracy in the West and its suppression in the East. It is also a reminder that the trade unions, despite their limitations, have been one of the great democratising movements of the last hundred and fifty years and remain crucial to any meaningful process of democratisation in the developing world.

Rounding off, our Forum feature presents two stimulating reflections on the issue of New Labour and its inheritance—socialist, social-democratic but also, Robert Taylor suggests, neo-Conservative—which has generated so much discussion in recent years. Our thanks to both Robert Taylor and Mark Bevir for these contributions. Thanks also to our expanded editorial board and team of editorial advisers, who also reflect the breadth of treatment and perspective which we see as being encompassed by the journal's title. The tenth in the series 'Books to be remembered' will appear in issue 28.

Readers are reminded that further details regarding *Rethinking Social Democracy*, including its Sheffield conference scheduled for April 2006, can be found at http://www.fssl.man.ac.uk/rsd. We also draw attention again to the journal's new website http://www.socialist-history-journal.org.uk and invite comments, commentary and feedback.

Socialist History Titles

Requests for back issues to ro@riversoram.demon.co.uk

Previous issues of *Socialist History* include:

Communism, Social Democracy and the Democracy Gap

Stefan Berger

In the twentieth century, debates about social democracy have been framed by the question of transforming or reforming capitalism. This has been the case for both the political and the academic debate. Politicians on the left have been arguing over this question and academics, most of them left of centre, have been debating the merits of various transformatory and reforming strategies. That this should have been the case is largely due to the victory of the Bolsheviks in the Soviet Union in 1917 and the subsequent creation of strong communist parties and eventually communist regimes in many parts of the world. Lenin's twenty-one conditions for admission to the new Communist International split social-democratic parties in most European countries and the subsequent dichotomy of social-democratic and communist parties became a defining characteristic of the short twentieth century.[1] Of course, not all social-democratic parties called themselves social-democratic. But the French Socialists, the British Labour Party and the German Social Democrats all subscribed to a recognisable set of ideas which made them join the Labour and Socialist International and which set them apart from the Comintern. Important differences of degree were sometimes reflected in the names that these working-class parties gave to themselves, but in the greater order of things they can all be classified as social-democratic, not the least in that they came to form the main opposition to the communist parties within the spectrum of the left.

This dichotomy of communism and social democracy came to dominate the terms of the debate about the left in the twentieth century.[2] Communists and communist historiography accused the social democrats of betraying working-class interests by abandoning the ultimate goal of transforming capitalism. Social democrats and social-democratic historiography in turn sought to justify alternative ways of imagining a society which combined state intervention and markets in order to achieve a more centralised distribution of resources and provision of life chances. Both communists and social democrats were predominantly concerned with the delivery of more social equality from the top downwards. Both were arguing about the best means of achieving that goal. Consequently much of the twentieth-century debate between communism and social democracy was about social and economic systems—a kind of hostile dialogue about which economic order would benefit the greatest number of people in human society.[3]

Capitalism determined the discursive patterning of the debate. Other issues had to take a back seat. Arguably democracy was one of the issues which the left neglected to discuss thoroughly. In 1919 Sidney Webb argued that 'socialists have contributed so far very little to the theory or practice of democracy'.[4] Seventy-six years later, Will Hutton could still write: 'Democracy or reforming the structure of the state never ranked high on the socialist wish list.'[5] A thorough comparative analysis of the engagement of communist and social-democratic parties with the concept and theory of democracy would undoubtedly reveal important differences between different parties, but it is my contention here that everywhere debates about democracy had to follow the framework set by the debates on capitalism. Even the lapsed communist Arthur Rosenberg, who famously attempted to write the history of 150 years of socialism under the analytical framework of 'Socialism and Democracy' could not escape this discursive patterning. Rosenberg distinguished between socialist democracy and various forms of bourgeois democracies. A socialist democracy was defined by its ultimate desire to abolish capitalism and introduce the self-government of the masses. By contrast, social democracy, for Rosenberg, was one of the four types of bourgeois democracy. While it strove for the political emancipation of the working classes, it did not question the existence of private ownership of the means of production. Hence it was closer to the other three types of bourgeois democracy: imperialist (England), liberal (Switzerland, Norway) and colonial (Canada) democracies.[6] And of course, to name but one more influential example, Max Horkheimer's famous dictum: 'Whoever does not want to talk about capitalism should also be quiet about fascism' (*Wer vom Kapitalismus nicht reden will, sollte auch vom Faschismus schweigen*) also reads: Whoever wants to talk about democracy (or any political system, for that matter), also has to talk about capitalism. Not only Marxist historians and politicians started from the assumption that the economic system determined politics; it was a contention shared by many of those bourgeois social historians who employed Max Weber's social theory in the writing of their histories. They too believed that social and economic change determined political change. The rise of poststructuralism and of a new political history in the 1980s and 1990s has criticised such assumptions and instead emphasised the autonomy of political processes and the constructedness of concepts and ideas employed to understand the world. But for much of the twentieth century, communist and social-democratic historiographies shared the firm belief in the existence of such links between a primary economic order and a secondary political system.

If capitalism was the linchpin of the debate, communists and social democrats and their respective historiographies also debated the merits and meanings of 'democracy'. Both ideologies attempted to claim the idea of democracy for themselves. Communists tended to start from Marx's distinction between bourgeois and proletarian democracy.[7] In the French revolution of 1848, Marx argued, the two concepts of democracy had parted company for the very first time. Bourgeois democracy rested on the twin pillars of the individual rights and freedoms and the rule of law. Democracy here was a formal mechanism of interest representation. Proletarian democracy started from the assumption that the formal democratic mechanisms had to be filled with social content. Furthermore, political democracy was in need of being supplemented by the democratisation of power relationships in the economy and in society as a whole. Representative democracy restricted to the political sphere would eventually give way to participatory democracy in as many fields of society as possible. In later years, the council democracy of the Paris Commune was to provide a model for Marx's understanding of a genuine proletarian democracy.[8] For Marx such a participatory democracy would make the state the servant of genuine human needs. In this respect, Marxism proved the mirror opposite of Hegelian state philosophy.

Marx also introduced the term 'dictatorship of the proletariat' which subsequently gave rise to much misunderstanding. Marx did not use the term to suggest the abolition of democratic republicanism. Rather he used it to describe the proletarian democracy of the future. According to Marx, all democracies were based on class rule. The democratic republic was the most advanced political organisation of bourgeois society. It provided the ground on which the class struggle of the proletariat could best succeed. Marx broke decisively with the conspiratorialism of those he deemed utopian socialists. Proletarian democracy would be established after the revolution, and it would not do away with a democratic republic. Only the context and content of that republic would change. However, Marx's championing of a 'dictatorship of the proletariat' lent itself to misconstruction, especially as he never bothered to think through systematically the question of the social organisation of democracy.[9] Lenin's Bolsheviks justified their rejection of liberal democratic rule and representative democracy with reference to the need for a distinct period of a 'dictatorship of the proletariat' in which the old class society would be overcome. The Bolsheviks could do that in the name of vanguardism, i.e. the idea that their party, a small minority of revolutionaries, had the theoretical means and insights to direct the working classes and act in their name and interest. Once the classless society was created and a harmony of interests existed, several political parties were unnecessary, as no antagonistic interests needed representation. Real democracy now consisted in the vigorous defence of the interests of the workers and farmers by the communist party. Political discussion and debate took place only in the leading institutions of that party. The democratic rights of the people, as enshrined for example in Stalin's constitution of 1936, were a mere sham.[10] The gap between the official communist discourse of democracy and the reality of harsh suppression of ideas which did not find favour with the leaders of the communist party was increasingly obvious to all those who wanted to see.

Social democrats were keen to point out the absence of basic democratic rights under communism and in fact often argued that the dictatorial nature of communism brought it close to fascism. Both regimes were different sides of a coin named totalitarianism. Social democrats were keen to present themselves as heirs to the nineteenth-century democrats who had fought hard to overcome the legacy of liberalism. Education and property should no longer define citizenship. Electoral reform became the watchword of social democrats across Europe, as they sought to provide access of the greatest number of people to the political sphere. Also taking their cue from the Marxist debates about class formation, they firmly believed that the working classes would ultimately form the vast majority of the overall population. It was the task of the social democrats to educate these workers and thereby contribute to the development of class consciousness. This process of education by what clearly was also a vanguard could best be done by a highly centralised and bureaucratised national party. Class-conscious workers would then vote for this party which in turn would allow it to capture the state. Capturing the state was perceived as the precondition for establishing a different economic and social system and, increasingly, for reforming capitalism. The widespread belief among West European social democrats that the capture of state power through the ballot box would inevitably lead to socialism contributed to the endorsement of an uncritical statism among the stalwarts of Second International socialism. Socialism would begin as soon as the social-democratic representatives of the working class had captured the state apparatus. Kautskyanism, Bernsteinan revisionism, Fabianism and most variants of continental Marxist thought were united in this belief in statism.

Democratic institutions

Democracy was thus primarily a means to an end. As the Eisenach programme of the German SDAP (Social-Democratic Workers' Party) put it in 1869, 'political freedom is the most indispensable precondition for the economic emancipation of the working classes. Hence the social question is indivisible from the political question. The solution to the former is conditional on the solution of the latter, and possible only in the democratic state.'[11] Political democracy was the means to achieve social equality. When Eduard Bernstein begged to differ and argued that 'in the last instance, for me, socialism means democracy, self-administration',[12] many in his own party declined to follow him. With Kautsky they continued to believe that the existing class society made any true democracy impossible. Yet democratic institutions in the class state facilitated class conflict and thus heightened class consciousness. They paved the way to the proletarian revolution which, in democratic states such as Britain and Germany post-1918, would eventually come about by peaceful means, i.e. through the ballot box. Hence it is not surprising that Kautsky's 'democratic Marxism'[13] was opposed to transferring the Bolshevik experiment to western Europe. Given that Kautsky nowhere specifically analysed the exact nature of the democratic transition from capitalism to socialism, his idea of democracy remained largely focused on parliamentary representation and the championing of the rights of the individual. It is generally noticeable that late nineteenth-century Marxist social democratic movements paid little attention to minutiae of democracy and democratisation. After all, practically all of them (to varying degrees) struggled rather with the absence of democratic structures. Hence they sought to bring democratic institutions about rather than marvel about the intricate problems of democratic systems.[14]

Nevertheless, one could argue that Kautsky, Bernstein's main adversary in the revisionism debate, was, rather ironically, as committed to liberal democratic thought as his ideological enemy. Both adhered to the belief that political democracy was the normative precondition for the development of a socialist society. Bernstein and Kautsky both championed the concept of representative democracy over that of direct democracy.[15] In that respect they were following Kant and Mill rather than Rousseau, and both were influenced by the rights-based political language of British constitutional theory. Yet Bernstein undoubtedly paid greater attention to the intricate problems of democratisation and linked democracy more firmly to socialism than most other contemporary Marxists including Kautsky.

The European-wide debate on revisionism revealed the strong commitment of social-democratic leaders in other Marxist parties to representative forms of democracy. MacDonald saw in Bernstein, who was a close personal friend, an intellectual mentor.[16] The French socialist Jean JaurËs, like Bernstein, was convinced that republicanism and democracy were eternally progressing to all fields of society. And he called on his fellow social democrats to engage constructively in the political process, to build alliances with other parties and other classes so as to further the aims of social democracy in specific policy areas.[17] The Swedish SAP (Social-Democratic Workers' Party) had, of course, its own version of Bernstein in the figure of Hjalmar Branting, who, unlike Bernstein, was almost undisputed leader of his party from its inception to 1925. Antonio Labriola, the 'father of Italian Marxism', argued in favour of a step-by-step introduction of social reform which would extend the democratic idea and build on existing democratic institutions.[18]

The democratic state

In the Weimar Republic the young German democracy had no firmer champion than social democracy. The 1921 Görlitz programme pledged allegiance to the 'democratic republic'. Rudolf Hilferding's theory of 'organised capitalism' perceived democracy as the specific state form of the working class. Like his mentor Kautsky, Hilferding upheld the notion that democracy was the basic precondition for the socialist transformation of society.[19] Social-democratic constitutional theorists such as Gustav Radbruch and Hermann Heller contributed signficantly to the theory of democracy in the 1920s.[20] They insisted on the centrality of the rule of law in protecting all citizens from the encroachment of the state onto the territory of their individual rights. In the inter-war years both the Soviet Union and a variety of fascist regimes served as powerful reminders of the importance of the constitutional democratic state for the social-democratic project. In his autobiography, looking back onto his experience as justice minister in the Weimar Republic, Radbruch was disappointed that he and his likes were unable to commit social democrats even more firmly to the democratic state: 'The masses had to be told firmly that democracy realises one half of the Social Democratic programme and that it had to be the primary consideration to stabilise what had been won.'[21]

Elsewhere, it had been easier to commit social democracy to championing the liberal-democratic state. During the Giolittian period before the First World War, the parliamentary party of the PSI was firmly committed to the parliamentary road to socialism.[22] In Spain the PSOE put all its energy into achieving a liberal-democratic state after forging an alliance with the Republicans in 1910. Subsequently important leaders of the party, such as

Indalecio Prieto, rallied to the modernisation and regeneration of Spain under liberal-democratic (but capitalist) conditions.[23] The British Labour Party after 1918 followed the teachings of MacDonald and the Webbs. Its MPs were totally committed to the parliamentary road to socialism.[24] The Swedish SAP moved from a self-declared working-class party to a people's party already in the 1920s—using Per Albin Hanson's notion of the people's home (*folkhemmet*) as crucial ideological tool.[25] The Dutch Social Democratic Party (SDAP) dropped its commitment to Marxism in 1937. Instead of endorsing the class struggle, the SDAP cited social reform and the preservation of democracy as the party's most important aims.[26] But also in countries well-known for their more illiberal traditions, social democrats often held up the values of liberal democracy. In July 1933 Otto Bauer called on fellow Austrian socialists not to lose sight of the fact that the establishment of a dictatorship of the proletariat was out of the question amidst rising fascist dictatorships. Instead, he argued: 'the decision will be made today not between democracy and the dictatorship of the proletariat, but between democracy and the dictatorship of fascism'.[27] Especially in the inter-war period a range of unstable democracies re-enforced the general concern of social democrats with class and the class struggle rather than with democracy *per se*. A relentless class struggle from above seemed to destroy bourgeois democracy in many of the newly founded democratic regimes of central and eastern Europe. Could bourgeois democracy therefore ever deliver socialism? Many social democrats continued to cling to this belief, although significant minorities within social-democratic parties had different views. Ultimately the united and popular fronts of the 1930s were all based on the lowest common denominator: a defence of parliamentary democracy against the advancing forces of fascism.

In the more stable conditions under the post-1945 Pax Americana in western Europe, social-democratic notions of democracy became limited to parliamentary representation, the rule of law and the championing of the rights of the individual. In particular the Swedish road to socialism now became a model for many social democrats in western Europe. The Swedish SAP was arguably the first and most successful social-democratic party to accept and practise pluralist democratic power politics in the early 1930s. They had forged an important alliance with the Agrarian Party (representing largely agricultural interests) and, while in government, began to experiment with Keynesian anti-cyclical economic policies. Within the framework of the liberal constitutional order and the democratic state, Swedish social democrats set out to manage capitalism more effectively and produce a 'capitalism with a human face'. The SAP was convinced that democracy and cross-class alliances were the key to a socialist society of the future. Its leading theoreticians, such as Branting, Ernst Wigforss and Per Edvin Sköld were also its leading politicians, and they shared a fundamental belief in the liberal democratic state's ability to deliver socialism.

If the communist notion of democracy was the thinnest of fig leaves for dictatorship, the social-democratic notion of democracy became increasingly narrowed down to liberal versions of representative democracy. What increasingly moved out of sight between the dominant communist and social-democratic historiographies were notions of democracy that had been present among groups of socialists who did neither fit the communist nor the social-democratic paradigm. To start off with, there is the history of the early labour movement which preceded the setting up of 'proper' social-democratic parties. This history is all too often treated as a mere pre-history in the communist and social-democratic narratives. Yet theirs is often a different history from that of the later mass socialist parties. In Britain, for example, the radical working-class Chartist organisations of the 1830s and 1840s formulated aspirations for a more democratic polity which were taken up by some socialist groups in the closing decades of the nineteenth century but became marginal within the mainstream Labour Party after 1906.[28] In Germany Thomas Welskopp has only recently restored the early history of social democracy to a history in its own right. He emphasised throughout that early social democracy was part and parcel of a democratic and national-revolutionary people's movement. The commitment of its members to intra-organisational democracy with agreed written procedures and elected committees was second to none. In their associational culture they practised an active citizenship and saw such active citizenship as the key to self-fulfilment.[29] Similarly, Maurice Agulhon has shown for the early French labour movement how workers in their associations, clubs and societies shaped their own public sphere and articulated a wide array of social, political and cultural concerns.[30] The early labour movement in Europe, sections of which stood condemned by no lesser gods than Marx and Engels as utopian socialists, did develop ideas about communitarianism, co-operation and self-management which have been largely ignored by social-democratic histories. They also often preached and practised the liberation of women and a radical gender politics which would often not be matched by the left until the late twentieth century.[31]

Some of these early nineteenth-century traditions survived and were further developed by the anarcho-syndicalist traditions of direct industrial action and workers' self-organisation. Paradoxically, some anarchist circles at the same time continued to practice strict conspiratorialism which was built on authoritarian rule and tended to disregard democratic procedure in every respect. Others championed the broadest measure of participatory democracy in local small-case communities of sovereign individuals who would at best co-operate in voluntary larger federations, ideally without developing intricate forms of representations. Overall, the anarcho-syndicalist mistrust and rejection of all centralist organisations and institutions, including political parties, parliaments, church and state stood in marked contrast to both the social-democratic and communist traditions.[32] In the revolutionary period between 1917 and 1923 council republics were the aim of a number of socialist revolutionaries in central and eastern Europe. They were informed by notions of a more radical and more direct democracy which often went hand in hand with demands for greater control over MPs, championing of plebiscites and referenda as well as suggestions for the rotation principle in leadership which would prevent the kind of hero-worshipping which was so prominent in social-democratic and communist organisations. After the First World War, left socialists formed a distinct group between communists and social democrats. A number of parties joined neither the Comintern nor the Labour and Socialist International, but, in 1921, set up the International Workers' Union of Socialist Parties, also known as 'Vienna Union'. Throughout the 1920s and 1930s a string of independent socialists defied the stark dichotomies between communist dogmatism and social-democratic reformism. Often it is among this group that we find the most interesting ideas concerning democracy. Democracy was not just seen as a political process but a mechanism of decision-making and balancing out conflicting interests which needed implementing at all levels of society. The key question was not about political power but about social power. Democratic processes needed to be adopted in all power relationships—in the family, at the workplace, in neighbourhood groups and even in the army. Ideas about industrial democracy, workers' control, socialisation and workers' self-management were particularly prominent among left-wing socialists who refused to commit themselves either to the reformism of social democracy or the undemocratic antics of the communists.

Particular emphasis was often put on the democratisation of the economic sphere. Calls for economic democracy became popular in the inter-war period and were adopted even by many social-democratic parties in the inter-war period. In Germany, the idea was developed by Fritz Naphtali, the head of the ADGB's (General Federation of German Trade Unions) Research Institute for Economic Affairs between 1925 and 1928. The democratisation of the economic sphere was to be achieved through extending the powers of works councils and establishing institutions for economic self-administration in which unions would be represented on equal terms with the employers. While the first steps towards 'economic democracy' could already be achieved under capitalism (essentially through state intervention in central processes of economic decision-making), full 'economic democracy', Naphtali insisted, would only be possible in a socialist economy. Hence the transformation of capitalism and the abolition of the private ownership of the means of production remained the long-term aim of the ADGB.[33] The Dutch SDAP also demanded a significant improvement in worker participation in management at the end of the First World War.[34] Whitley councils in Britain after 1918 as well as the Mond-Turner talks in the late 1920s signalled an interest in economic democracy among sections of the British labour movement as did the more theoretical contributions of Webb, Cole and Harold Laski.[35] In France, Jaurès had already argued that the political democracy of the republic had to be extended to the whole of the country's economic life.[36]

Yet, despite the popularity of demands for economic democracy even among mainstream social democrats, it is among groups of left-wing social democrats, independent socialists, guild socialists, anarcho-syndicalists and unorthodox communists that we find most concern for the fostering of a democratic civil society in the inter-war period. Statism of the communist or social-democratic variant, they argued, neglected the problem of social power and did not actively seek to empower working people in their everyday lives. People had to practice democracy on a daily basis rather than delegate responsibility for decision-making to elected representatives or a party vanguard. They had to be encouraged to take control of their lives in a more direct way. Localised direct democracies in which the people could realise democracy in all spheres of life were to be preferred to the deadening weight of heavily bureaucratised parties, trade unions and states. Rosa Luxemburg's opposition to Leninism was rooted, above all, in different ideas about the democratic organisation of society.

After 1956

In the post-Second World War period many of these concerns surfaced again with the post-1956 emergence of the first New Left, with the advances of the student movement in the 1960s, with second-wave feminism, with the growth of green/ecological movements in the 1970s and with the revival of notions of active citizenship in communitarian thought in the 1980s and 1990s. 1956 brought various attempts in Eastern Europe to democratise the Stalinised people's democracies. Reforms went furthest in Poland and

Hungary and included economic, cultural and political liberalisation as well as experiments with grassroots democracy which eventually resulted in the declaration of a multi-party state in Hungary on 30 October and the withdrawal of Hungary from the Warsaw Pact on 1 November 1956. In western Europe, the invasion of Hungary by Warsaw pact troops on 4 November 1956 and the swift restoration of a dogmatic communist regime at long last loosened the bonds of large sections of the intellectual left to the Soviet Union and the communist project in eastern Europe. The critique of Stalinism in the west went together with a continuing commitment to anti-capitalism which made left intellectuals explore alternative routes to overcoming the capitalist systems of the west. E. P. Thompson's concerns with the morality (rather than the economics) of capitalism and his emphasis on the lived experience of workers under capitalism were a direct reaction to his rethinking of communism in the wake of 1956. His concern for the agency of working people was also a concern with the ways in which people organised their everyday lives.[37]

In the 1960s the students were enamoured by Max Horkheimer's attacks on 'integral statism' (*integraler Etatismus*), a concept first put forward in Horkheimer's Californian exile in 1942. He argued that the 'authoritarian state', whether of the capitalist or communist variant, had perfected its power mechanisms to such a degree that it could function without reference to open terror. In capitalist states, social-democratic parties and trade unions had become part and parcel of the authoritarian state. These former interest organisations of workers had reduced notions of progress to the advancement of state capitalism. The real enemy of Horkheimer's forceful essay was bureaucracy and the bureaucratic state. The aim was to create spaces for individuals to make decisions about their lives which are not predetermined by overpowerful and centralised bureaucracies.[38] The significance of 1968 for the left in Europe lay in its championing of anti-authoritarianism and its formulation of a new democratic politics of the everyday which declared proudly that the personal was the political. It highlighted the agency that people had over their lives and contrasted such practices of self-actualisation with the alienation produced by passive consumerism.[39] At the universities students experimented with new democratic forms of teaching and learning. In the wake of the student rebellion of the 1960s we also witness the birth of a strong feminist movement. One of its key concerns was the liberation of women who arguably suffered most from the authoritarian regulation of gender relations. Women's liberation movements sprang up across western Europe and, organised in small localised groups committed to democratic procedure, co-ordinated imaginative campaigns for the legalisation of abortion and against a wide array of discriminatory and degrading practices directed against women. Giving women the rights over their own bodies (reproductive rights) as well as access to jobs, equal pay and generally access to social and political power, these were among the most important demands made by feminists, and all of them were closely related to questions of democracy.[40]

The Green movement picked up the criticisms of communist and social-democratic notions of progress that had been voiced by left-wing dissenters in the 1950s and 1960s. Quality of life, they argued, could not be measured simply in terms of maximising economic growth levels and rising consumption levels. Such progress had led to alienating forms of consumerism and to the ruthless exploitation of nature. It had brought the planet to the brink of global self-destruction. What was urgently needed was a search for new ways of constructing social communities and collective identities. The Greens cherished the anti-authoritarian counter-culture of 1968 and aimed to support projects which breathed the air of participatory democracy and direct action connected to the student rebellion of the 1960s. As parties they found it difficult to accept strong organisational and bureaucratised structures and preferred more informal and loose organisations which often showed an ingrained hostility against forms of leadership and officialdom. Their rejection of consumerism found expression in a formulation of a specific post-materialist political agenda which succeeded in making significant inroads into a variety of European electorates in the 1980s and 1990s.[41] A variety of Green thinkers attempted to give often very different answers to the central question of reconfiguring humanity's relationship to the natural environment and of democratising the everyday life of citizens across Europe.[42]

Communitarian thinkers, not unlike Green theorists, also started from the assumption that people need to be freed from the tutelage of large central organisations. The social order envisaged by communitarians often involved small decentralised communities in which individuals know each other and interact with each other on a basis of shared norms and values.[43] Communitarian thinkers have criticised social democrats and communists for being one-sidedly concerned with how to optimise the equal distribution of resources. In doing so, they neglected the central question of involving the people in decision-making processes about such allocations of resources. This is also why the traditional left has been incapable of putting forward a convincing theory of political democracy which puts the active engagement of citizens centre stage. Instead it created a nanny state which produced welfare dependencies and the passive endurance of vast sections of the underprivileged of the increasingly diminishing welfare benefits shared out by an impoverished state struggling with successive economic crises. The necessary reduction of the public sector, communitarians argued, needs to go hand in hand with the encouragement of more active forms of citizenship, where people are enabled to take control over their lives. This is only possible where diverse forms of social exclusion are effectively overcome. New social-democratic thought, and in particular that of the British Labour Party, has drawn extensively from communitarian thinking on citizenship.[44]

Throughout the twentieth century minority traditions within the left have shown a remarkable appreciation of and concern with the problems of the democratic organisations of society, an appreciation that was largely (although never entirely) absent from the communist and social-democratic mainstreams. Today, at the beginning of the twenty-first century, the dichotomies between communism and social democracy which structured the last century have gone. Class has long ceased to be dominant cleavage in European politics. Capitalism is the name of the global economic order, and its adversary in the form of the anti-globalisation movement is a curious mixture of anti-movements which lack both coherence and convincing alternatives.

Which democracy?

It is beyond doubt that communism has been a huge failure: it could not create a viable social and economic system; it often could not even fulfil the basic needs of its populations. More to the point, for the purposes of this essay, communism failed to develop democratic procedures which would have given it legitimacy among wider sections of the population. Instead it relied on centralised bureaucracies which stifled innovation and wasted human and natural resources on a grand scale. By comparison social democracy has been a remarkable success story. Western Europe changed fundamentally over the course of the twentieth century. Social-democratic principles of equality, welfare and state intervention in markets helped to make it a better place for the overwhelming majority of the population. Outrageous inequalities of consumption still exist, but even the poorer section of the population have been given access to resources to a hitherto unprecedented degree. The social democratisation of West European politics came to a crushing halt in the 1980s. Neo-liberalism swept everything before it and portrayed three of the four pillars of the old social-democratic self-understanding as key evils which had caused the economic crisis of the 1970s: statism, Keynesian economics and the welfare state now all stood condemned. The only pillar which was left largely intact was the commitment of social democracy to democracy. Democracy seemed indeed, in the words of Paul Hirst, 'socialism's best reply to the right'.[45] But a statement such as this only brings us full circle and returns us to the question: which democracy?

At the beginning of the twenty-first century the project of democracy needs rethinking. In the 1990s there was much talk about growing disillusionment of voters with political parties which found expression in lower and lower participation rates in elections. Increasing numbers of citizens withdrew even from the limited sphere in which they had previously been active: the ballot box. Their passivity seemed to threaten the legitimacy of representative democracies. Arguably this development was also related to the one-sidedness of the social-democratic concern with providing the citizens with adequate resources and protecting them from the vagaries of the market. Such statist policies imposed both rights and duties on passive citizens and produced a state-directive collectivism. Politics and political processes became increasingly removed from the everyday lives of citizens. They were hardly involved in the systems of institutions meant to ensure protection against arbitrary rule. If freedom has to be institutionalised, arguably it is institutionalised too much today. Power has been carried out too much on behalf of citizens rather than by them. In fact, an activation and politicisation of citizens was often explicitly avoided, as high levels of politicisation were perceived as dangerous for political stability. Joseph Schumpeter, in his influential exploration of the relationship between capitalism, socialism and democracy of 1942 argued that people tended to act irrationally. They could not be trusted to make rational, or, for that matter, moral choices.[46] A fugitive from European fascism, Schumpeter felt attracted to theories of crowd psychology, and the victory of fascism in many European states in the interwar period cast a long shadow over democratic theories in the post-war era. To many, like Schumpeter, it seemed best to leave politics to the reasonable democratic elites. The people were asked nothing more than to vote every couple of years.

Arguably the expansion of citizenship rights pushed forward by social democracy throughout the twentieth century did not always include the propagation of more active forms of citizenship. In the 1960s and 1970s some on the left had already argued that the representative democracies in the West resembled 'thin democracies'.[47] Today these democracies are in need of addressing the crucial question of how to engender a more active sense of citizenship in its populations. Citizenship has to become less of a status and more of an active practice and experience. Yet citizens have to be made: they need resources, especially education, knowledge and experience, and the continued existence of hierarchic and authoritarian structures in society form a distinct hindrance to the possibility of democratic learning.[48]

A variety of often quite diverse contemporary thinkers have at least begun to address this problem of involving more people in decision-making processes,[49] and a transformed social democracy is struggling with the task of addressing some of the key issues outlined above.[50] Thus, for example, the concern with democratisation is a central ingredient of Anthony Giddens's 'third way'. In his historical analysis, Giddens comes to the conclusion that 'socialism is closely tied up with ideals of democracy... Reformist socialism...has accepted the importance of democracy for socialist goals...Democracy essentially offers a framework within which socialist parties can peacefully rise to power and implement their programme of change.'[51] Indeed social democracy's record, as far as democratisation is concerned, has been considerable. They contributed vitally to a strengthening of parliamentary democracy, not the least through franchise reforms. They fortified a public sphere upholding public freedoms. They championed a civil society which expanded workers' rights. They fought for the legal recognition of trade unions, reinforced civil liberties and built up welfare legislation entrenching social rights. Not a mean record by any stretch of the imagination.

And yet the concern of contemporary analysts, like Giddens, is for the need for a further 'democratisation of democracy'. He calls on the left to go beyond orthodox liberal democracy and experiment with extending democracy to more social spheres. Ultimately, Giddens argues, democratisation may well be the key means to enhance social cohesion in western societies.[52] Calls for 'democratising democracy' and 'second-wave democratisation' abound in Giddens's 'third way' publications. Decentralisation of political decision making, constitutional reform (devolution), administrative efficiency, less bureaucracy, local direct democracy and more active citizens' involvement describe 'a form of government which it should be the aim of social democrats to promote: the new democratic state.'[53] Giddens was, of course, not the first political philosopher on the left to put democracy centre stage. Margaret Thatcher was just celebrating her third subsequent election victory, when John Keane suggested that the crisis-ridden socialist tradition could be revitalised by reference to democratic theory. His self-declared aim was to show 'how the meaning of socialism can and must be altered radically—into a synonym for the democratisation of civil society and the state'.[54] Equally, albeit with different emphases, Jörgen Habermas has argued at length that socialism needs to be rethought in liberal-democratic terms. His theory of communicative action is still at the basis of how citizens can seek consensus and achieve communal fraternity.[55] But, more recently, Habermas has also stressed the importance of liberal freedoms and bourgeois rights. After all, Habermas maintains, the question of how power is organised is not solved by decisions on who holds power. Therefore the law becomes the central element in upholding a precarious balance of interests in democratically constituted societies.[56]

In the twenty-first century the left needs to turn around the order of things. Social democracy needs to be rebuilt from its democratic foundations. In what arguably amounts to the most spirited defence of the ambitions of the European left and, at the same time, the most trenchant critique of its failures, Geoff Eley has recently argued from a Marxist perspective that, 'by identifying "the Left" not with socialism but with a more capacious and exacting framework of democracy, in all its appropriate social, economic, cultural and personal dimensions, the disabling implications of the crises of socialism during the last third of the twentieth century might be brought under control'.[57] In my view, this is fundamentally correct and represents the most fruitful perspective from which to write the history of the left today. Eley, who, in many respects, attempts to rewrite Rosenberg's history of the relationship between democracy and socialism for the twenty-first century, places much emphasis on democracy's desire to transform capitalism. While this is undoubtedly a legitimate angle to take, at the same time it is a very traditional angle. For eventually, Eley, like so many writers of the left before him, thereby upholds the superiority of the socio-economic over the democratic. Characteristically, throughout the book, he shies away from precise definitions of what he understands by democracy. Problematically, Eley links advances in democracy to a revolutionary perspective: 'the most important gains for democracy have only ever be attained through revolution'.[58] There are sparks of revolutionary romanticism, when he writes that 'there remains something uniquely inspiring in the spectacle of masses of people in political motion, collectively engaging the future'.[59] Yet in the introduction, where Eley talks about democracy, he almost exclusively talks about liberal understandings of democracy and the rule of law. From a liberal understanding of democracy, the left of course had many allies among European left liberals and Christian Democrats who also sought to extend democracy to broader sections of the population. Characteristically, Eley at two points actually includes Christian Democracy among his understanding of the left —without, however, even beginning to discuss the bases of Christian-Democratic politics in post-war Europe.[60] If Eley is willing to admit at times that social democrats have contributed significantly to the advances of democracy in twentieth-century Europe, he tends to be dismissive of their reformism and parliamentarism at other points in the book. Thus, for example, the 'constitutionalisation' of social-democratic parties in the inter-war period is portrayed one-sidedly as a conservative plot to blunt working-class radicalism.[61] Reformist parties like the British Labour Party 'remained stuck in a parliamentarist groove' in the 1980s,[62] as though parliamentary politics mattered little. At the same time as dismissing what has been crucial to the democratic self-understanding of social democrats, Eley shows remarkable sympathies for the communist project, despite having to admit that the Soviet model had purged socialism of democracy.[63] Creative energies and intellectual potential are time and time again primarily located in western communism, Eurocommunism and thereafter in the new social movements, whereas social democracy at best earns the begrudging respect of the author.

Yet, however much one might differ with this particular take on the left, ultimately Eley is right: the history of the left as a motor of democratic advances in the nineteenth and twentieth centuries 'needs to be recovered and given its due'.[64] It has to be recovered precisely because the left has always underplayed that aspect of its history as one part in the greater struggle to either tame or overcome capitalism. A thorough discussion of democracy though, in my view, needs to be disentangled from debates about socio-economic systems. Of course the economic sub-system of society needs to be democratised as well, and capitalism has been and continues to be a major obstacle on that road. Hence anti-capitalism as a break on democracy is a viable critique for the left. But democracy is a deeper and more important project than overcoming the economic system of capitalism. Democracy needs to be given true primacy before tired debates of social and economic transformation. The German sociologist, sometime adviser to Chancellor Gerhard Schröder and veteran-68er Oskar Negt has recently argued, 'a public debate about democracy and socialism—would be a first important step towards solving the identity crisis of the left'.[65] Why a first step, I am tempted to ask? Let a discussion of democracy and socialism be the decisive step towards a different identity of the left which at long last puts to rest its one-sided fixation with economics. The left cannot 'exit' from its own history,[66] but it can begin to tell different stories about its past which will influence the way in which it can build the future.

Notes

1. Eric Hobsbawm, *Age of Extremes. The short twentieth century 1914–1991* (London, 1994).
2. Geoff Eley, 'Reviewing the socialist tradition', in Christiane Lemke and Gary Marks (eds), *The Crisis of Socialism in Europe* (Durham, 1992), pp.21–60.
3. For masterly comparative surveys of the European left in the twentieth century see Donald Sassoon, *One Hundred Years of Socialism. The West European left in the twentieth century* (London, 1996), and Stefano Bartolini, *The Political*

Mobilisation of the European Left 1860–1980. The class cleavage (Cambridge, 2000).

4. Sidney Webb, 'A Stratified Democracy', supplement to the *New Commonwealth*, 28 November 1919, p.2.

5. Will Hutton, *The State We're In* (London, 1995), p.48.

6. Arthur Rosenberg, *Demokratie und Sozialismus* (1938; Frankfurt am Main, 1962 edn), pp.302ff; see also English edition, *Democracy and Socialism. A contribution to the political history of the past 150 years* (London, 1939).

7. Karl Marx, *The Eighteenth Brumaire of Louis Bonaparte* (London, 1954 edn).

8. A. Demirovi, 'Marx und die Aporien der Demokratietheorie', *Das Argument*, vol. 30 (1988), pp.847–60.

9. Uwe-Jens Heuer, 'Demokratie/Diktatur des Proletariats', in: Wolfgang Fritz Haug (ed.), *Historisch-Kritisches Wörterbuch des Marxismus*, vol. 2 (Berlin, 1995), pp.534–51.

10. Iring Fetscher, *Von Marx zur Sowjetideologie. Darstellung, Kritik und Dokumentation des sowjetischen, jugoslawischen und chinesischen Marxismus* (Frankfurt am Main, 1977), pp.132–8.

11. Dieter Dowe (ed.), *Programmatische Dokumente der deutschen Sozialdemokratie* (Berlin, 1984 edn), p.174.

12. Cited in Manfred B. Steger, *The Quest for Evolutionary Socialism: Eduard Bernstein and Social Democracy* (Cambridge, 1997), p.140.

13. Dick Geary, *Karl Kautsky* (Manchester, 1987), p.78.

14. Anton Pelinka, *Social Democratic Parties in Europe* (New York, 1983), p.14.

15. Kautsky was instrumental in defeating the German socialist apostle of direct democracy, Moritz Rittinghausen, whom he attacked vigorously after 1893. For Rittinghausen's ideas on direct democracy see Moritz Rittinghausen, *Die direkte Gesetzgebung durch das Volk*, (Cologne, 1877 edn). For Kautsky's rejection of Rittinghausen see Karl Kautsky, *Der Parlamentarismus, die Volksgesetzgebung und die Sozialdemokratie* (Stuttgart, 1893).

16. David Marquand, *Ramsay MacDonald* (London, 1977), pp.56ff., 164.

17. On Jaurès see Leszek Kolakowski, *Main Currents of Marxism. Its Rise, Growth and Dissolution*, vol. 2 (Oxford, 1978), pp.129ff.

18. Luigi Dal Pane, *Antonio Labriola nella Politica e nella Cultura Italiana* (Turin, 1975).

19. F. Peter Wagner, *Rudolf Hilferding: Theory and Politics of Democratic Socialism* (Atlantic Highlands, 1996).

20. Hermann Heller, 'Staat, Nation und Sozialdemokratie' (1925), in Heller, *Gesammelte Schriften* (Leiden, 1971), pp.527–42.

21. Gustav Radbruch, *Der innere Weg. Aufriß meines Lebens* (Göttingen, 1961 edn), p.131.

22. Toby Abse, 'Italy', in Stefan Berger and David Broughton (eds), *The Force of Labour* (Oxford, 1995), pp.145ff.

23. Angel Smith, 'Spaniards, Catalans and Basques: Labour and the Challenge of Nationalism in Spain', in Stefan Berger and Angel Smith (eds), *Nationalism, Labour and Ethnicity, c. 1870–1939* (Manchester, 1999), pp.74ff.

24. Ralph Miliband, *Parliamentary Socialism* (London, 1961).

25. Sheri Berman, *The Social Democratic Moment. Ideas and Politics in the Making of Inter-War Europe* (Cambridge, MA, 1998), ch.7.

26. Dietrich Orlow, *Common Destiny. A Comparative History of the Dutch, French and German Social Democratic Parties, 1945–1969* (Oxford, 2000), p.21.

27. Otto Bauer, 'Um die Demokratie', *Der Kampf*, vol.26 (July 1933), p.270, cited Gerd-Rainer Horn, *European Socialists Respond to Fascism. Ideology, activism and contingency in the 1930s* (Oxford, 1996), p.22.

28. Logie Barrow and Ian Bullock, *Democratic Ideas and the British Labour Movement, 1880–1914* (Cambridge, 1996).

29. Thomas Welskopp, *Das Banner der Brüderlichkeit. Die deutsche Sozialdemokratie vom Vormärz bis zum Sozialistengesetz* (Bonn, 2000).

30. Maurice Agulhon, *The Republic of the Village: The People of the Var from the French Revolution to the Second Republic* (Cambridge, 1982).

31. Pamela Pilbeam, *French Socialists Before Marx. Workers, Women and the Social Question in France* (Teddington, 2000), especially ch.6 on the 'new woman'.

32. Marcel van der Linden and Wayne Thorpe (eds), *Revolutionary Syndicalism: An International Perspective* (Amsterdam, 1989); David Goodway (ed.), *Anarchism: History, Theory and Practice* (London, 1989).

33. John Moses, 'The Concept of Economic Democracy within the German Socialist Trade Unions during the Weimar Republic', *Labor History*, 34 (1978), pp.45–57.

34. Lex Heerma van Voss, 'The Netherlands', in Berger and Broughton, *Force*, p.50.

35. Jutta Rabenschlag-Kräußlich, *Parität statt Klassenkampf? Zur Organisation des Arbeitsmarkts und Domestizierung des Arbeitskampfs in Deutschland und England 1900–1918* (Frankfurt am Main, 1983); Michael Dintenfass, 'The Politics of Producers' Co-operation: the FBI-TUC-NCEO Talks 1929–1933', in John Turner (ed.), *Businessmen and Politics. Studies of business activity in British politics, 1900–1945* (London, 1984).

36. Kolakowski, *Main Currents*, vol.2, p.130.

37. See, for example E. P. Thompson, *The Communism of William Morris: A lecture by Edward Thompson given on 4th May 1949 in the Hall of the Art Workers' Guild, London* (London, 1965), p.18.

38. Max Horkheimer, 'Autoritärer Staat', in: Horkheimer, *Gesellschaft im Übergang* (Frankfurt am Main, 1981).

39. Ronald Fraser, et al., *1968: A Student Generation in Revolt* (New York, 1988); David Caute, *The Year of the Barricades: A Journey through 1968* (New York, 1988).

40. Monica Threlfall (ed.), *Mapping the Women's Movement: Feminist Politics and Social Transformation in the North* (London, 1996).

41. Gerassimos Moschonas, *In the Name of Social Democracy. The Great Transformation: 1945 to the Present* (London, 2002), pp.154–6.

42. Alan Scott, *Ideology and the New Social Movements* (London, 1990).

43. Michael Taylor, *Community, Anarchy and Liberty* (Cambridge, 1982); Amitai Etzioni, *The New Golden Rule. Community and morality in a democratic society* (New York, 1997).

44. Andrew Gamble and Anthony Wright (eds), *The New Social Democracy* (Oxford, 1999); Lothar Funk (ed.), *The Economics and Politics of the Third Way* (Hamburg, 1999).

45. Paul Hirst, 'Democracy: Socialism's Best Reply to the Right', in Barry Hindess (ed.), *Reactions to the Right* (London, 1990), p.161.
46. Joseph Schumpeter, *Capitalism, Socialism and Democracy* (New York, 1942).
47. Benjamin R. Barber, *Strong Democracy. Participatory politics for a New Age* (Berkeley, CA, 1984); see also Philip Green, *Retrieving Democracy* (London, 1985).
48. Adrian Oldfield, 'Citizenship: An Unnatural Practice'?', in: *Political Quarterly*, vol.61 (1990), pp.177–87.
49. Edmund Neill, 'British political thought in the 1990s', in: Stefan Berger (ed.), 'Labour and Social History in Great Britain: Historiographical Reviews and Agendas 1990 to the Present', *Mitteilungsblatt des Instituts für soziale Bewegungen*, vol.28 (2002), pp.167–84.
50. Herbert Kitschelt, *The Transformation of European Social Democracy* (Cambridge, 1994).
51. Anthony Giddens, *Beyond Left and Right. The future of radical politics* (Cambridge, 1994), pp.59, 62.
52. Giddens, *Beyond Left and Right*, pp.104–33.
53. Anthony Giddens, *The Third Way. The renewal of social democracy* (Cambridge, 1998), pp.70–7, and Giddens, *The Third Way and its Critics* (Cambridge, 2000), pp.58ff.
54. John Keane, *Democracy and Civil Society. On the predicaments of European socialism, the prospects for democracy and the problem of controlling social and political power* (London, 1987), p.xiii.
55. Jürgen Habermas, *The Theory of Communicative Action*, 2 vols (New York, 1989); see also Axel Honneth and Hans Joas (eds), *Communicative Action. Essays on Jürgen Habermas's Theory of Communicative Action* (Harvard, 1991).
56. Jürgen Habermas, *Faktizität und Geltung. Beiträge zur Diskurstheorie des Rechts und des demokratischen Rechtsstaats* (Frankfurt am Main, 1992).
57. Geoff Eley, *Forging Democracy. The History of the Left in Europe, 1850–2000* (Oxford, 2002), p.503.
58. Eley, *Forging Democracy*, p.x.
59. Eley, *Forging Democracy*, p.x.
60. Eley, *Forging Democracy*, pp.289, 492.
61. Eley, *Forging Democracy*, p.241.
62. Eley, *Forging Democracy*, p.464.
63. Eley, *Forging Democracy*, p.306.
64. Eley, *Forging Democracy*, p.10.
65. Oskar Negt, *Achtundsechzig. Politische Intellektuelle und die Macht* (Frankfurt am Main, 1998), p.166; also pp.135ff. for a discussion of 'new forms of democratic participation'.
66. Moschonas, *In the Name*, p.329 concludes that 'Social Democracy is ready to "exit" from its own history'.

Reasons for 'Progressive' Disunity
Labour and Liberal politics in Britain, 1918–45

Andrew Thorpe

The Labour Party was, by some distance, the most significant political organisation of the left in twentieth-century Britain. Over the century as a whole, on every meaningful measure—electoral success, periods in government at both national and local levels, membership, and wider social and cultural impact—it dwarfed its rivals. This might lead us to believe that we can understand all that we need to know about Labour by looking at it alone. And yet the party's history cannot be understood fully without attention to the place of the party in relation to other political parties and movements. To a large extent, the Labour Party was made and remade, not just by itself, but by the actions of the other organisations with which it was competing.

Some important work has been done in this area. Some significant features and characteristics of the Labour Party have been highlighted by means of a focus on the borders and barriers between the Labour Party and movements to its left, be they the Communist Party, the Independent Labour Party, independent Marxist movements, or entryist organisations like the Militant Tendency, even though we still await an authoritative study of the relationship between Labour and the far left. In February 2004, Labour's disaffiliation of the Rail, Maritime and Transport union (RMT) for supporting Scottish Socialist Party candidates—in contravention of Labour Party rules—provided a further example of the Labour-far left interface arousing interest.[1] Some people have celebrated this strong line against communists and the like, seeing it as a 'frontier guard' against undesirable elements; some have even regretted that the process did not go further.[2] But others have regretted the extent to which Labour erected barriers against the far left. They have taken the view that the British left as a whole would have been stronger if it had been more united, and less riven by sectarian divisions on what they see as essentially secondary issues. This 'missed opportunity' view has, implicitly at least, influenced quite a few observers.[3]

The notion that there were real possibilities of profitable Labour co-operation with the far left appears, to most people, like a throwback to a bygone age today. The collapse of communism has largely silenced that section of the far left that still claimed adherence to aspects of the Soviet tradition. Marxist critics of the Soviet tradition, however, have largely failed to show people that they have a convincing alternative. Thus while there are those who still purport to see great opportunities ahead for the radical left, it would probably be fair to say that they are in more of a minority than ever.

In more recent years, however, greater attention has been paid to the idea that the missed opportunity came, not in Labour's relations with those to its political left, but with those to its political right. It is not hard to see why this should have been the case. The revival, from the 1970s, of third-party/centre-party politics in Britain was matched by increasing interest in the opportunities for realignment of 'progressive' forces of the centre-left. Now, there was increasing focus on the idea that the conscious erection of barriers to co-operation between Labour and the Liberals was a wilful act of political sectarianism which caused huge problems, not least the division of the radical forces in British politics and, consequently, the creation, almost by default, of a long period of Conservative hegemony. Perhaps the most significant single act in this process was Labour's adoption, in 1918, of a new party constitution which in effect declared Labour a socialist party. Far from being a natural development arising from Labour's 'coming of age', this constitution reinforced, even invented, obstacles to Lib-Lab co-operation. And those obstacles, in turn, helped to ensconce the Conservatives in power for virtually the whole of the inter-war period, and to give them a flying start in the competition for votes at most elections thereafter.[4] On this reading, the fault lay very largely with those who are seen as having wilfully obstructed the continuation of the 'progressive alliance' after the First World War. After all, as David Blaazer has ably demonstrated, there was no shortage of advocates of a wider unity after 1918.[5]

Such a view was, of course, given a huge boost by wider developments in the 1980s and 1990s. The end of the Cold War and the collapse of communism in all but its most remotest hideouts, the apparent removal of socialism from the political menu, and the reining in of militant trade unionism under years of Conservative government, all combined to remove sticking points between Labour and those to its immediate political right. Those obstacles were not entirely removed, as it transpired, but at times it did appear as though they might be: in particular, Labour's leader from 1994 onwards, Tony Blair, did on many occasions stress his belief that his personal politics, and those of the 'New' Labour party which he was leading, derived not just from Labour's own history, but from a broader 'progressive' tradition which included Liberals every bit as much as Labourites. In his speech to the Fabian Society celebrating the fiftieth anniversary of Labour's 1945 election victory, Blair stressed the need to 'value the contribution of [the Liberals] Lloyd George, Beveridge and Keynes and not just [the Labourites] Attlee, Bevan or Crosland', as well as calling on his party's members 'to welcome the radical left-of-centre tradition outside our own party, as well as celebrating the achievements of that tradition within it'.[6] To some extent, this can be seen as a clever re-application of an old Labour tactic—flattering Liberal traditions in order, not to promote real top-level co-operation, but to appeal to Liberals, over the heads of their leaders, to vote Labour. Nonetheless, the fact that Blair took the process to such significant lengths, including even a series of clandestine meetings with the Liberal Democrat leader, Paddy Ashdown, about a possible coalition, suggests that he was, in the period up to the 1997 election at least, convinced by the case for a renewed 'progressive alliance'.[7]

At the same time, there was renewed focus in historical writing on the earlier period of 'progressive alliance'. Since the 1980s, much of the most important work on the politics of the two or three decades before 1914 has tended to stress the continuities of progressive politics in Edwardian Britain. In the place of older, 'heroic' visions, which had represented the coming of the Labour Party as the culmination, and inevitable by-product, of the rise of the working class, this new work emphasised the contingent nature of Labour's pre-war advance; the continuing vitality of the Liberal Party and Liberalism; and the extent to which the two parties were still able to muddle along together in a largely informal, but nonetheless real, 'Progressive Alliance'.[8]

Of course, no serious historians or commentators have suggested that it would have been easy to keep the alliance in being. Perhaps the most spirited advocate of the possibilities for continuing Lib-Lab collaboration has been David Marquand. But his *The Progressive Dilemma*, first published in 1991, is as nuanced as one would expect from someone who could interpret the subject from the differing perspectives of the historian, the political scientist, and the political practitioner. This article does not seek to act as a direct critique of Marquand's work: those seeking such a critique are directed to the excellent piece published by Fielding and McHugh in 2003.[9] Rather, I am concerned here to argue, on the basis of research conducted on all levels of both parties, that the obstacles to co-operation in the period between 1918 and 1945 were even greater than has been generally recognised. They were, in fact, so significant as effectively to rule out Lib-Lab collaboration, let alone any kind of 'progressive alliance'.

Liberal-Labour relations 1914–45: an outline

Argument has continued, and will continue, about the extent to which the 'progressive alliance' was fracturing prior to 1914. But it is beyond doubt that it did not survive the Great War. Liberal progressivism was becalmed, not least because its main cabinet advocate, David Lloyd George, was sucked into the war effort, first as Chancellor of the Exchequer, then as Minister of Munitions and Secretary of State for War, before he effectively broke with the Liberal Party altogether to become Prime Minister of a Coalition government in December 1916.[10] Many other progressive Liberals were marginalized by their criticism of the war. The result was that the less progressive elements of the party, which in reality had never entirely lost control, now reasserted themselves strongly. Labour's hopes were raised by the expansion of trade union membership, and by an apparently increased appetite, and potential, for increased state power. At the same time, the fears of at least some of its leaders were stirred by the introduction of compulsory military service, and talk of industrial conscription, as well as by the development of radical, anti-democratic revolutionary movements in Russia after the February Revolution of 1917. Many of Labour's leaders now expected some kind of swing to the left to take place after the war. In one sense, of course, they welcomed this: it clearly offered opportunities to them. However, they also saw that the divided and discredited Liberals were in no state even to try to exploit the expected leftwards surge. If Labour, therefore, did not step into the breach, then the moment might well be seized by the far left, revolutionaries who had no interest in the kind of 'ordered progress' which characterised the thinking of Labour's leading strategists and intellectuals, but would instead bring bloody insurrection in their wake.[11] Accordingly, those strategists supported the adoption of a new party constitution in 1918. This constitution gave the trade unions, as a whole, more influence over the party than ever before.[12] But it also declared the intention of building up the party in every part of Britain, through the introduction of constituency Labour parties with individual membership; and, most famously in retrospect, it committed the party to socialism (although the word itself was not used) through what was to become known as 'Clause IV': the commitment to 'the common ownership of the means of production'. The adoption of a socialist commitment was notable in the context of this paper because it marked, and was meant to mark, a clear dividing line with the Liberals: a line that Liberals could not cross, without becoming socialists and thereby renouncing their Liberalism. It was made clear that Liberals who did make this renunciation would be welcome. But it was equally clear that they must come in on Labour's, and not their own, terms. In the contemporary Communist parlance, what Labour was seeking was not a united front from above, involving deals between Labour and Liberal leaders, but a kind of united front from below, wherein ordinary Liberals would move towards Labour leaving the Liberal leadership isolated.

And, of course, many Liberals did make such a move. No undergraduate essay on the subject is complete without the requisite list of often rather grand names: C. P. Trevelyan, E. D. Morel, Arthur Ponsonby, Viscount Haldane, H. B. Lees-Smith.[13] However, the high hopes of 1917–18, which had led to the promulgation of the new constitution, were soon being scaled back. Economic slump from August 1920, and the subsequent—and consequent—series of severe industrial defeats suffered by the trade unions, dented the party's aspirations. The development of a bloody Communist dictatorship in Russia did little to ease the task of Labour politicians and canvassers when challenged about 'Red Scares'; the weakness of the British Communist Party poked fun at suggestions that a commitment to socialism had been necessary to head off a potent threat from the far left.[14] The Conservatives' decision to jettison Lloyd George's activist and interventionist leadership and settle instead for the role of party of 'resistance'[15] made them formidable opponents in a polity which had had enough of overseas adventures, which was busy remembering and memorialising its war dead, and where for many there was no more potent cry than the desire to return to 1913.[16] In this context, far from being the advantage that had been hoped, it might well be that Labour's radical departure of 1918 was, in fact, an obstacle to its progress. Indeed, it is not *entirely* idle to speculate whether, had it not adopted a socialist commitment in 1918, Labour would have done so at any point from mid-1920 onwards.

This, in turn, raises the question of whether there was more potential for Labour-Liberal co-operation between 1918 and 1945. It should be borne in mind, of course, that there were periods of co-operation between the two parties in this period. In January 1924, for example, they united in the House of Commons to turn out Stanley Baldwin's protectionist Conservative government following the latter's loss of its parliamentary majority at the general election of December 1923. The first Labour government, which followed, relied on the Liberals to remain in office, especially so as the Conservatives remained the largest party in the House of Commons. However, that support was withdrawn over MacDonald's poor handling of the Campbell Case later in 1924, and the government fell. At the general election that followed, the Liberals probably suffered more than Labour from the 'Red Scare' atmosphere, since those voters who took such things seriously were now more likely to support the party of resistance—the Conservatives—than the Liberals who had let the 'socialists' into office in the first place.

Both Labourites and Conservatives hoped that the Liberals' heavy defeat in 1924 would lead to their imminent demise and the clarity of a two-party system. But such hopes were temporarily dashed by the Liberal revival under Lloyd George, who took over as leader from the ailing former Prime Minister, the Earl of Oxford (H. H. Asquith) in October 1926. The Liberals' advance between then and the 1929 general election was not enough to bring them to parity with Labour (which emerged as the largest party for the first time) or the Conservatives, but it was sufficient to give them the balance of power in the House of Commons once more. This time, the Liberals tried to wield the balance of power more cleverly, but the Conservatives' effective refusal to bargain with them meant that they were forced, by early 1930, into fairly steady support for the Labour government, despite the latter's many failings.[17] From mid-1930 onwards, there were regular meetings between Labour ministers and Liberal leaders, and rumours were flying in the spring of 1931 that a Liberal might soon join the cabinet. Although some historians have taken these signals very seriously, others have been less convinced that a Lib-Lab coalition was about to emerge: it seems more likely that the combination of a joint desire to avoid a general election and a sense of drift in the government combined to produce a fertile ground for rumours.[18]

In any case, hopes of a renewal of some kind of progressive alliance were confounded in the summer of 1931. The decision of the Liberals to back the Conservatives in calling for heavy spending cuts to meet a projected budget deficit that August led to the creation of the National government under Labour's erstwhile leader, Ramsay MacDonald. And that government then went on to trounce Labour at the October 1931 general election, winning 554 seats to Labour's 46. The National government remained in office—under first MacDonald, then Baldwin, and then Neville Chamberlain—until 1940. The Liberal MPs split, more or less in half (in addition, Lloyd George—who had opposed the National government at the election—and three members of his family formed a separate 'family group'). The Liberal Nationals remained part of the government throughout, finally merging with the Conservatives in the late 1940s.[19] The official Liberals, first under Sir Herbert Samuel (1931–35) and Sir Archibald Sinclair (1935–45) remained in the government until 1932, and finally moved onto the opposition benches in November 1933. By the latter date, however, they were in sharp decline. There were, arguably, some signs of a slight recovery in the later 1930s, but these came, ultimately, to very little; while fleeting hopes of progress in the Second World War were to be bitterly disappointed by the party's virtual obliteration at the 1945 general election.[20] At that election, the Liberals won only 12 seats. Labour, on the other hand, won 393, and formed its first majority government with a parliamentary majority of 146. Although there had been some local-level co-operation in anti-Conservative fronts in the later 1930s, based on the popular front agitation,[21] and although Labour and the Liberals had been partners under Churchill in the 1940–45 Coalition government, the two parties remained separate. Indeed, the results of the 1945 election seemed finally to bear out the promise of the formal separation that had taken place in 1918: the strategy of keeping the Liberals at arm's length had, it seemed, finally paid off.

Obstacles to co-operation

Nineteen forty-five, then, seemed to vindicate Labour's strategy towards the Liberals over the past generation. But as the party failed to establish itself as the natural party of government after its great post-war administration (1945–51), so doubts began to arise once more. During the 1970s and 1980s, these doubts began to be expressed with increasing stridency. Why could not there have been greater co-operation against the Conservatives, in such a way as to shut the latter out from power at the national level? Inevitably, given the polarising nature of the Thatcher administration between 1979 and 1990, and the growth of the idea that a more ecumenical approach towards anti-Conservative politics would be of benefit, such questions began to be asked with increasing urgency. As people began, for example, to consider the merits of 'tactical voting' to remove Thatcher, so they also began to pay attention to the question of whether the decades-long 'division' of anti-Conservative progressive forces had not been a mistake.[22]

Counterfactuals are always intriguing, and frequently tempting. But the notion that it was possible to maintain any kind of 'progressive unity' after 1918 rests on shaky foundations. In almost every respect, in fact, there were severe obstacles to co-operation between Labour and the Liberals by 1918. These operated at the levels of leadership; ideology; policy; trade unionism; relations with the Conservative Party; and organisation and ethos. To demonstrate the point, each of these areas will be discussed in turn.

Leadership attitudes were one clear hindrance to greater co-operation. Most Labour leaders of the period shared something of a distrust of the Liberals. This had not prevented co-operation before 1914, but it had tended to limit it, and its intensification after 1914 was palpable. The dominant figures of the inter-war Labour Party, certainly, had a degree of prejudice against the Liberals. Among the key leaders during the 1920s, MacDonald and Arthur Henderson had both been disappointed by the Liberals' failure to adopt them as candidates in the 1890s, perhaps more so in the former case than the latter.[23] Neither had refused to work with the Liberals before the war as a result; MacDonald, indeed, had been involved with some leading progressive Liberal thinkers in the London-based discussion group, the Rainbow Circle.[24] But it seems plausible to argue that, as the Liberal Party as a whole moved away from progressivism, so the party's less palatable elements returned to the fore. Certainly, Labour's frequent criticisms of the character of those elected as Coalition Liberal MPs in 1918 would suggest that they were only comfortable with a certain type of Liberal. Henderson had respected Asquith, but such respect had been dented by the events of the Great War, and, as his post-war performance deteriorated, he could be forgiven for seeing him as yesterday's man.[25] MacDonald, for his part, 'had never had a high opinion of Asquith'.[26] The relations of both men with Lloyd George deteriorated considerably during the war, and still more during his post-war premiership (1918–22), when Labour's progress owed much to its stern critique of the Coalition's record on a variety of issues.[27] Of all the Liberal leaders prior to 1931, Samuel was the one with whom they found it easiest to do business: he was the most pro-Labour of Liberal leaders, having, for example, shown some sympathy to the miners' cause in 1925–26, and attempted to act as an arbitrator during the General Strike of 1926. It is not surprising that it was Samuel's name that was mentioned most frequently in gossip about which Liberal might enter the Labour cabinet in 1930–1.[28] Other leading Labourites of the 1920s, even if moderates, were not necessarily interested in working with the Liberals: J. H. Thomas, for example, was in many ways more like a Conservative than a Liberal.[29] Perhaps Philip Snowden, Chancellor of the Exchequer in the first two Labour governments, came closest among the party's leading figures in the 1920s to supporting cross-party co-operation. After his breaks with Labour in 1931 and the National government in 1932, indeed, he gravitated towards the Liberals, broadcasting for them at the 1935 election and, according to some accounts, living out his days in receipt of a pension from Lloyd George.[30] But Snowden was in some ways a more marginal figure in the development of Labour's political strategy in the 1920s than his position as Chancellor of the Exchequer in the first two Labour governments might suggest; and his inability to build coalitions within the party around the positions he favoured meant that there was no prospect whatever of his overturning the prevailing strategy in favour of a closer relationship between Labour and the Liberals.

If Labour's leaders down to 1931 did not feel much empathy with the Liberal Party, then it is hardly surprising that their successors were even less enthusiastic. Someone like Henderson, born in 1863, or MacDonald, born three years later, had grown into middle age with the Liberal Party as a key element of British politics: they had been thirty-one and twenty-eight years old respectively when William Gladstone had finally retired from the premiership in 1894, forty-three and forty when the Liberals won their great victory in 1906. For their successors—people like Clement Attlee (born 1883), Hugh Dalton (1887), or Herbert Morrison (1888)—the Liberals conjured up less resonant memories: less the glory days of Gladstone than the dog days of Asquith. Nor did they feel much enthusiasm for contemporary Liberal leaders—Samuel had burnt his boats with Labour by finally siding with the National government in 1931 and remaining in it as it trounced Labour at that year's general election, while after 1935 Sinclair was generally seen as an amiable but somewhat lightweight individual leading a by now doomed party.[31] The other notable leading Liberal of the period was Sir William Beveridge, who shot into the party leadership in late 1944 following his election as MP for Berwick: but, for all Labour's apparent enthusiasm for the Beveridge Report of 1942, there was a good deal of personal distrust of someone who was generally regarded, in Labour circles, as a very difficult colleague: 'full of egoism and petulance' was Dalton's view in May 1942.[32] In short, there was very little room for collaboration between the leaders of the two parties during this period as a whole.

Another major obstacle was ideology. It might be suggested that this should not have mattered: that the concerns of the here-and-now should have taken priority over somewhat theological questions regarding the ultimate fate of private property, and so on. But this is a rather misconstrued criticism. Labourites and Liberals were 'ideological' whether they liked it or not. Ideology is not an optional extra in politics, but is fundamental to it: even those who would proclaim themselves as un-ideological are thereby subscribing to an ideology.[33] And, in any case, both Labour and the Liberals *did* like it: they took ideology seriously. It was valuable in itself, as offering *raisons d'etre* for each party. It also had strategic value, in helping to keep each party together in times of crisis, of which there were many between the wars. Like all ideologies, the Liberals' Liberalism and Labour's socialism were not unchanging: and as Michael Freeden reminds us, 'in their multiple metamorphoses, the differences between ideological families are unceasingly accentuated or moderated. That is the give and take of political discourse, relating to institutional and social environments that, in turn, encourage convergence or divergence.'[34] But they were not adaptable enough in this period to allow sufficient convergence to make a 'progressive alliance' a reality.

Liberals were not modest in their claims for their ideology. They believed that Liberalism was an honourable doctrine that had liberated people from age-old shackles, enabling them to enjoy a freer existence. The notion that this could or should be given up, or even compromised, was anathema for most. Indeed, reading through Liberal politicians' private correspondence and public writings, and the records of the party at all levels down to the humblest local party associations, what is clear during this period is the pride that such people still took in being Liberals. Their political world might seem to have been falling apart, but they were not, on the whole, interested in changing their views if this meant renouncing Liberalism. On the contrary, they believed that the reason that the world had become a worse place since 1914 was precisely *because* people had neglected the basic Liberal values of the former generation: as one liberal body put it in March 1940, '[t][he world ha[d] indeed become a nightmare since it turned its back on Liberalism following the Great War'.[35] Linked with this was an imperturbable optimism on the part of some Liberals, an extreme example being the Chairman of East Dorset Liberal Association who stated on 29 August 1939—three days before Germany attacked Poland to unleash almost six years of bloody and genocidal war in Europe—that 'there was a wave of Liberalism spreading over Europe, and the Liberal creed was being adopted in other Parties and other countries'.[36] Even the Liberal Nationals, who remained with the Conservatives in the National government after 1932, were keen, at least until the end of the Second World War, to sustain an image of themselves *as* Liberals *within* a broader National alliance. After the Munich agreement, the Liberal National cabinet minister Sir John Simon wrote to the prominent Liberal J. A. Spender bemoaning the attitude taken up by 'the Opposition Liberal rump in the Commons. Anyone would think they had never heard of Asquith'.[37] Similarly, the Liberal MP Herbert Holdsworth, on moving from the Liberals to the Liberal Nationals in 1938, emphasised that he had never deviated from any Liberal principle, adding 'I still claim to be as good a Liberal as ever I was & intend to remain a Liberal'; but he was 'not going to obey the decision of a little caucus'.[38] They might be allies of the Conservatives, but they were not merely Conservative stooges. If even the Liberal Nationals continued to feel such a bond to Liberalism, then it is hard to imagine that the independent Liberals would have felt any less of a commitment; and that, in turn, calls into serious question the extent to which they might have participated willingly in any kind of 'progressive' movement. It also suggests that any idea of giving up on Liberalism would have been even weaker in the 1920s, when the party's activists and supporters could still convince themselves that the party had the chance of a future in government in the short term.

But it was not just that Liberalism mattered to Liberals. It was also that socialism mattered to Labourites. Indeed, it almost certainly mattered to more Labourites—taken as a whole—in this period than it had before the Great War. Those of a leftish disposition had, to a large extent, seen that war as proving the benefits and merits of socialism. For all, the February revolution in Russia had been an inspiration: and even if most did not want to repeat the Bolshevik revolution in all its details, many were impressed by the potential for rapid socialist transformation which they believed Soviet Russia possessed. But even where they were more sceptical about the Soviet regime, they felt that the national and international problems that had been thrown up by the war could only be resolved by significant social change, and socialism was an integral part of their analysis. There might have been an element of calculation in the adoption of the socialist commitment in 1918, but that does not mean that the socialists in the party did not believe in it, or that they would have been happy to accept its dilution in the interests of appealing to Liberals. Indeed, the 1922 party conference passed unanimously a resolution denouncing 'any alliance or electoral arrangement with any section of the Liberal or Conservative Parties', with Sidney Webb telling delegates 'very emphatically' that it would be 'a terrible mistake' for Labour to try to enter government with any other party.[39] Freeden has suggested that '[t]he argument that many differences between evolutionary socialism and left-liberalism are illusory is a compelling one'.[40] But even if this was the case, it must be remembered that the sub-sets he mentions— 'evolutionary socialism' and 'left-liberalism'—did not in any way comprise the whole of Labour's socialism or the Liberals' Liberalism in the period.

In any case, the division operated at the level of policy as well as that of ideology; and this, again, clearly constrained the potential for co-operation. During the Edwardian period there had been considerable policy overlaps: the defence of free trade against Chamberlainite protectionism, advocacy of Irish Home Rule, support for 'the people' against 'the peers', commitment to a degree of social reform, desire for the clarification of trade unions' legal position, and an inclination towards temperance, among others, had provided a raft of areas on which there was the potential for broad—though never unanimous—agreement.[41] To be sure, within each of these areas there were differences of emphasis, but it was possible for these to be overcome, most of the time. Even on the vexed issue of the trade union political levy, where a Liberal railwayman, W. V. Osborne, provoked the eponymous legal judgment that called unions' payments to the Labour Party into question, a solution was eventually reached (by the 1913 Trade Unions Act) which, ultimately, produced about as much consensus as it was possible to produce.[42]

After 1918, though, the policy landscape was more divisive. The extension of the role and powers of the state during the war soon led to new fissures, or deepened old ones, between Liberals and Labourites. Most Labourites welcomed the state's expansion, although some, notably guild socialists, expressed concerns about an over-mighty state unchecked by other agencies.[43] Many Liberals were a good deal less sanguine, not just during the First World War, but right down to the end of the Second and, indeed, beyond. In some ways this might seem surprising, given the development of Liberal policy at various stages—towards the Yellow Book under Lloyd George in 1927–9, or the fulsome acceptance of Beveridge in the latter part of the Second World War. But appearances here were a little deceptive. During Lloyd George's period as leader (1926–31) there remained considerable—if at times subterranean—hostility towards the party's apparent conversion to statism.[44] As Garry Tregidga has argued, in the South West—one of the party's few remaining strongholds at the end of the 1920s—the Liberals were 'still sustained by the forces that had motivated the party before the war: a deep reverence for the cause of Gladstone, the moral fervour of religious nonconformity and a belief that the Liberals were still a potential party of government'.[45] The party's eager adoption of Beveridge—who was virtually its joint leader, with Sinclair, at the 1945 election—smacked of a degree of desperation, and it was this desperation which led Liberals largely to ignore, or fail to see, the extent to which, as Jose Harris has demonstrated, Beveridge himself had moved towards a socialist perspective at this time.[46] In particular, she argues, 'his view of "full employment" in 1942 was essentially a state socialist rather than a Keynesian conception'.[47] For all the noise that surrounded Beveridge—much of it, it must be said, made by Beveridge himself—there remained within the party a significant, though at this stage rather muted and cowed, opposition from those—like the banker Sir Andrew MacFadyean, or the editor of the *Huddersfield Examiner*, Elliott Dodds—who would have preferred greater emphasis on free enterprise, free trade, individual liberty, and the small trader.[48]

Emphasis on free enterprise also calls into question the issue of trade unionism. Here, the Liberals' often unfavourable attitudes were crucial in determining Labour hostility. It was true that, by and large, the Liberals had been more sympathetic than the Conservatives towards trade unions since the mid-nineteenth century. It was, after all, Conservative-appointed judges who were making the running against the unions in the 1890s and 1900s, and the Liberal government under Sir Henry Campbell-Bannerman that restored trade union legal immunities by means of the 1906 Trade Disputes Act. However, it is worth reiterating that the case that challenged the whole basis of Labour Party funding through the trade unions was brought by a working-class Liberal, in the person of Osborne (who was to remain active in local Liberal Party politics in Walthamstow right up to the time of the Second World War).[49] As stated above, the 1913 Act did resolve matters, but its failure simply to overturn Osborne was taken by some trade unionists as a clear sign of Liberal hostility, even though its long-term effects probably helped the Labour Party more than anyone had expected.[50] After the war, the conduct of the Lloyd George Coalition in crushing industrial disputes (such as the 1921 coal lockout) did much to fuel union hostility towards him and towards the Liberals who supported his Coalition.[51] This might not have mattered in terms of Liberal-Labour relations, except that the collapse of the Coalition eventually brought many such Coalitionists back into the Liberal Party proper. In 1926, ironically, it was Lloyd George among the Liberal leaders who attempted to take a conciliatory line in the General Strike; but the bulk of the Liberal leadership came out strongly on the side of the government and against the unions, and Sir John Simon, in particular, made a speech which challenged the legality of the Trades Union Congress's actions in calling the strike.[52] This speech 'had a swingeing effect on trade union headquarters' at the time, and was subsequently used, along with other Liberal arguments, by the Conservative government to help justify the 1927 Trade Disputes and Trade Unions Act, which was seen by the unions as a vindictive piece of class legislation, enacted in revenge for the General Strike.[53] Any attempt at a Labour-Liberal coalition in 1929–31 would have aroused strong union resistance, especially since the Liberals were lukewarm at best towards any repeal or amendment of the 1927 Act.[54] It is far from clear that there was any significant change in Liberal attitudes towards unions thereafter: certainly, trade unionists were not particularly conscious of any change.

This division, on an issue of fundamental importance for the Labour party, could not, and cannot, be wished away. Of course, it would be simplistic to say that Labour in this period was simply 'union-dominated'. But, at the same time, if enough unions felt sufficiently animated on a particular issue, they were usually able to block the party from taking a particular path. And this was always likely to be the case where any pact with the Liberals was concerned. It is certainly no coincidence that those Labourites who enjoyed the best relations with the Liberals in this period tended to be the ones, like Snowden, who were least enamoured of the unions. None of this, of course, is to suggest that either the unions or the Liberals were 'wrong' in the stances they took on this issue: but it does demonstrate how elusive any kind of agreement would have been likely to prove.

Such difficulties were also marked when it came to the Liberals' relationship with the Conservative Party. At the national level, their co-operation with the Conservatives in 1931 can be seen as something of an aberration for an otherwise progressive party. The official Liberal party, after all, had opposed the Lloyd George Coalition, and supported the first two Labour governments in parliament, at least up to a point. Samuel suggested to King George V the replacement of the National government with an alternative Liberal-Labour coalition under MacDonald shortly before the calling of the 1931 election. (The King's reaction appears to have been somewhat dismissive, to put it mildly.)[55] Sinclair eventually led the Liberals to come out against Chamberlain's appeasement policy, and his party was far less hostile than Labour in 1938–9 towards the idea of a broad alliance against the National government.[56] Radical policy alternatives emanated from the party from time to time, never more so than in the late 1920s.

And yet there were always other Liberalisms, even at national level. These Liberalisms were often disparate, and they had little in common with each other; some were pro-Lloyd George, some anti, and so on. But even when they stood outside the Liberal Party, such Liberalisms could never be ignored by the leadership of that party. And the one thing they did share was a strong, almost visceral hostility towards Labour and practically everything it stood for. Such Liberalisms included the Liberalisms of the Lloyd George Coalition in the early 1920s, of the anti-Lloyd George Liberal Council from 1926 onwards, of the Liberal Nationals in the 1930s and 1940s, and of the anti-statist defenders of 'the independent man' and small trader during the Second World War. This is a tradition which fits less easily with prevalent modern-day views of the Liberals as a 'progressive' party, and so has tended to be neglected by modern historians with Liberal sympathies: but it was no less strong for that. In industrial West Yorkshire, for example, the stolid business-oriented Liberalism identified by Jack Reynolds and Keith Laybourn prior to 1918 remained the predominant force during the period down to 1945.[57] Indeed, West Yorkshire provides some very good illustrations of the kaleidoscopic nature of local Liberalisms. Here, one such example—Huddersfield—will have to suffice. At the 1945 general election, the MP defending the seat was a Liberal National, Sir William Mabane, who had the support of the local Conservatives, but who was also the nominee of the official Huddersfield Liberal Association. He faced opposition from an official Sinclair Liberal candidate in the person of Roy Harrod, who was a fervent admirer of John Maynard Keynes, the progressive

Liberal economist. Yet the chairman of the independent Borough Liberal Association, which was supporting Harrod, was Elliott Dodds, who although a local figure was also, at national level, arguably the Liberal Party's chief advocate of the interests of small independent traders against the all-embracing claims of the state. Unsurprisingly, perhaps, Labour won the seat.[58]

This reminder that the national scene was not the only forum for Liberal-Labour relations is apposite. While the Liberals might flirt with Labour at national level, they often tended to cleave pretty firmly opposite direction at the local level. Of course, there were exceptions, but it was usually the case that, where Liberals responded to their increasing weakness in local councils by entering into inter-party pacts, it was not with Labour, but with the Conservatives. In the council chamber, the Liberals were, in many cases, every bit as much a 'party of resistance' as the Conservatives: resistance to high rates, to direct labour, to municipal trading, to council housing, and to all the other manifestations of municipal socialism. Anti-Labour pacts were formed in many towns and cities, such as Bristol and Sheffield.[59] To Labourites in such places, the idea of a national-level pact of any kind between Labour and the Liberals would have made no sense at all, and would, indeed, have aroused considerable criticism and hostility.

Issues of organisation and ethos formed another barrier between the parties. It might well be that the Edwardian period represented a unique concatenation of characteristics of the two parties' machines, in which there was, for once, the potential for close co-operation. On the one hand, the powerful, but broadly tolerant, Liberal machine was able to offer a nascent Labour Party—which was not yet strongly centralised on the model of continental social democratic parties—the opportunity of collaboration as a junior partner.[60] Many Liberals, and pro-Liberal historians, have regretted this: Roy Douglas, for example, wrote in 1971 that '[t]he price which was paid for the Liberal Whips' squeamish refusal to strangle the Labour Party in its cradle was the division and confusion of radicals throughout the inter-war years, and the eventual establishment of 'Labour' administrations which had remarkably little in common with the wishes and needs of the workers themselves'.[61] In the same year, the then Liberal leader, Jeremy Thorpe, argued that the pact had been 'an act of uncalled-for [Liberal] electoral generosity unforgivable in a Chief Whip'.[62] In the context of 1903, however, it made sense for the Liberals, who had been struggling in opposition for eight years, and trounced at the 1900 general election, to attempt an electoral deal with the new Labour organisation.[63] At the very least, they could thereby try to ensure that the coming election did not see the Conservatives returned to power for want of a united front against them. As stated above, this was feasible because there was such a degree of overlap in terms of policy between Labour and the Liberals.

As Labour's organisation grew, however, so its ethos began to harden in a way less favourable to these kind of inter-party deals. To be sure, a key development here was self-willed: namely, the adoption, in 1918, of the new party constitution, which ensconced the trade unions more firmly in control of the party than ever before (much to the chagrin of ILPers like Snowden).[64] But the second, which came two years later, was something about which Labour could have done very little: the formation of the Communist Party of Great Britain. These two events had a significant impact upon the way the Labour Party was organised and the way in which it saw co-operation with other organisations. In the specific context of relations with the Liberals, two points seem especially worthy of note. The first is that the party after 1918, still more than hitherto, had an ethos which was strongly influenced by trade union ideas of solidarity and loyalty to majority decisions. Such an ethos sat ill with the views of many Liberals. Even among those who came over to the Labour Party, some were to find it hard to knuckle down to accepting that ethos.[65] For example, Josiah Wedgwood came to be seen as a maverick figure: among other things, he was denied official party endorsement at the 1931 general election for refusing to accept the parliamentary Labour Party's new, more restrictive standing orders.[66] Sir Charles Trevelyan, for his part, was also refused official endorsement at that election, for the same reason; and he was to be expelled in 1939 for supporting Sir Stafford Cripps's campaign for Labour to enter a broader alliance against the National government.[67] For those who remained within the Liberal Party, ideas of co-operation with a party which, at least on the face of it, was so much committed to the collective over the individual was a real problem.[68] The second point concerns the communists. One of the key reasons for Labour's organisational tightening from the early 1920s onwards was a keen awareness of the threat that communists and communism posed to an essentially social democratic party. The chief aim of Labour's key strategists was to keep the communists out, and to do this they had to erect barriers against co-operation with *all* other parties. This made them, ultimately, as hostile towards collaboration with Liberals as they were regarding co-operation with communists. It is worth remembering, in this connexion, that Cripps, Trevelyan, Aneurin Bevan and others were expelled in early 1939 for advocating a broad front which would have included Liberals as well as communists.[69] But even had they advocated collaboration with the Liberals alone by this stage, they would probably have suffered some form of disciplinary action: Liberals were seen as undesirable in themselves, but it was also recognised by the party leadership that, once the Liberals had breached the barrier, it would have *then* been so much harder to keep the communists out.

Finally, the potential for co-operation had to rely on an assessment of the potential futures on offer. Once they had made the decision for independence, Labourites would have taken a lot of persuading that some kind of collaboration with the Liberals would have brought serious long-term benefits. According to the vague evolutionary beliefs which in some inchoate way helped to shape the thinking of most Labourites, Liberalism was an outdated ideology whose time—the nineteenth century—was passed; the ideology of the twentieth century was socialism. The increasingly obvious debility of the Liberal Party during the inter-war period did little to counter such prejudices. It is possible, of course, to argue that at certain points Liberal prospects looked a little brighter: this was true, say, of the time of the 1923 election; of the period between Lloyd George's accession to the leadership and the beginning of 1929; or, perhaps, the period around 1936 when the Liberal Party, under Sinclair, was beginning to reform itself (although the extent to which that represented a real revival must be very doubtful). For the most part, however, these were periods of at best fleeting, and often questionable, progress, set within a much wider context of decline and failure. In a sense it was a counsel of despair for Labourites to wish to harness themselves to such an obviously failing, and arguably doomed, organisation. There was plenty to despair about in Labour's performance during this period, but there was also much of which the party felt it could be proud, and the failure of the Liberal Party even seriously to arrest its decline in anything but the very shortest of terms made it an unlikely and unwelcome collaborator.

Conclusion

Viewed in global terms, it is easy to see why the period between the wars should have given rise to so much counterfactual wishful thinking. In the British context, the Conservative Party's domination of government at national level led many progressives, at the time and afterwards, to try to discover some alternative. At the time, many progressives did precisely that.[70] We should not simply dismiss the potential of their efforts: the politics of the period were not pre-ordained: there was usually some room for human agency. Politicians were not, and are not, merely helpless puppets within structures. However, they did have to operate according to constraints about which they could often do very little. Conversely, there were those in both parties who actively sought to diminish, and ultimately extinguish, any prospects for co-operation between the two parties. A combination of rational calculation, sectarianism, personal ambition, and sheer prejudice severely inhibited the prospects for those who sought to renew the Edwardian 'progressive alliance' in a new form. And yet that was not the whole story. The alliance had had its opponents in the pre-1914 period, after all, but the context then had been less favourable to those opponents, and the alliance had—more or less—survived. It was the change in the context, outlined above, that made the crucial difference to the prospects for co-operation. This, in turn, meant that the advocates of progressive unity—who remained numerous, and in some cases prominent—faced a tough, and ultimately futile, battle in trying to forge wider alliances.

It is worth concluding with two further—perhaps paradoxical—thoughts. One is that even had there been a progressive alliance, it would probably not have made any difference on the key question of Conservative hegemony. Simplistic analysis which assumes that Liberal-Labour co-operation would have led to all their voters combining straightforwardly against the Conservatives is not fit to be called psephology. There is clear evidence that such a deal would instead have led to the large-scale desertion of Liberals from 'progressivism' and into the Conservative camp—that was what happened, anyway, at almost every general election between the wars, even when the Liberals were fighting on an independent ticket. It might have been true, as it was during the 1980s, that there was an anti-Conservative majority among voters; but, as also at that time, there was even more markedly an anti-*Labour* majority.

The other point appears to contradict this, but in fact complements it. It is that the variety of 'lefts' on offer in the inter-war period was, in many ways, very rich. This was a period of weakness for the left at the macro level, but one where, in micro terms, it was relatively strong. There was great debate and discussion at all levels; there were differences of ideology that really did seem to matter. The nature of the post-1945 settlement—both in terms of what was included but also of what was excluded—was to some extent set during this earlier period. Perhaps, like Protestant non-conformity in the nineteenth century, the left was most vibrant on the ground when it was most divided. In this regard, ecumenical politics is perhaps rather like ecumenical religion: agreeable and inoffensive, but rarely very vital, usually quite bland, and almost always somewhat ineffectual in arresting decline.

Notes

1. 'RMT expelled from Labour Party', *Railnews*, 7 February 2004, http://www.rail-news.co.uk/displaynews.asp?ID=345, accessed 20 September 2004. Thanks for comments are due to Stefan Berger, John Callaghan, and Kevin Morgan; and for financial assistance to the Arts and Humanities Research Board, the British Academy, and the University of Exeter.

2. Austin Mitchell, *Four Years in the Death of the Labour Party* (London, 1983), p.28; Carl F. Brand, *The British Labour Party; A Short History* (Stanford, CA, 1965).

3. See especially Ralph Miliband, *Parliamentary Socialism: A Study in the Politics of Labour* (2nd edn, 1972), pp.216–20, 229–30.

4. The most developed version of this argument comes in David Marquand, *The Progressive Dilemma: From Lloyd George to Kinnock* (London, 1992 edn).

5. David Blaazer, *The Popular Front and the Progressive Tradition: Socialists, Liberals, and the Quest for Unity, 1884–1939* (Cambridge, 1992).

6. Tony Blair, speech to Fabian Society, 5 July 1995, reprinted in Tony Blair, *New Britain: My Vision of a Young Country* (London, 1996), p.7.

7. For these discussions, see especially Paddy Ashdown, *The Ashdown Diaries, Volume One: 1988–1997* (London, 2000).

8. See e.g. D. Tanner, *Political Change and the Labour Party, 1900–1918* (Cambridge, 1990); E. F. Biagini and A. J. Reid (eds), *Currents of Radicalism: Popular Radicalism, Organized Labour, and Party Politics in Britain, 1850–1914* (Cambridge, 1991).

9. Steven Fielding and Declan McHugh, '*The Progressive Dilemma* and the social democratic perspective', in John Callaghan, Steven Fielding and Steve Ludlam (eds), *Interpreting the Labour Party: Approaches to Labour Politics and History* (Manchester, 2003), pp.134–49.

10. Tanner, *Political Change and the Labour Party, 1900–1918*, pp.373–83.

11. On this see Andrew Thorpe, *A History of the British Labour Party* (2001 edn), pp. 27–40; J. M. Winter, 'Arthur Henderson, the Russian Revolution, and the reconstruction of the Labour Party', *Historical Journal* 15 (1972), p.755; A. Henderson, *The Aims of Labour* (Manchester, 1918 edn), pp.67–70.

12. Ross McKibbin, *The Evolution of the Labour Party, 1910–1924* (Oxford, 1974), pp.90–1.

13. Catherine Ann Cline, *Recruits to Labour: The British Labour Party 1914–1931* (Syracuse, NY, 1963) remains useful on this subject.

14. For the CPGB in this period, see Andrew Thorpe, *The British Communist Party and Moscow, 1919–1943* (Manchester, 2000).

15. Maurice Cowling, *The Impact of Labour, 1920–1924* (Cambridge, 1971), esp. pp.1–3.

16. For analysis of how these considerations held Labour back in rural areas in particular—where there had initially been high hopes of advance after 1918—see especially Nicholas Mansfield, *English Farmworkers and Local Patriotism, 1900–1930* (Aldershot, 2001), especially pp.159–98.

17. Philip Williamson, *National Crisis and National Government: British Politics, the*

Economy and Empire, 1926–1932 (Cambridge, 1992), pp.105–6, 109–14.

18. Williamson, *National Crisis and National Government*, pp.251–2, argues strongly for the possibility of a reconstruction along these lines; John Campbell, *Lloyd George: The Goat in the Wilderness, 1922–1931* (London, 1977), pp.294–6, and David Marquand, Ramsay MacDonald (London, 1977), pp.601–3, argue along broadly similar lines, although somewhat more circumspectly; Andrew Thorpe, *The British General Election of 1931* (Oxford, 1991), p.56, takes a different view.

19. For the Liberal Nationals, see Graham Goodlad, 'The Liberal Nationals 1931–40: the problems of party in a 'partnership government', *Historical Journal*, 38 (1995), pp.133–43.

20. Malcolm Baines, 'The survival of the British Liberal Party, 1932–59', Oxford D. Phil., 1990; see also his published work: 'The survival of the British Liberal Party, 1933–59', in A. Gorst, L. Johnman and W. S. Lucas (eds), *Contemporary British History 1931–1961: Politics and the Limits of Policy* (1991), pp.17–32, and 'The Liberal Party and the 1945 general election', Contemporary Record, 9 (1995), pp.48–61.

21. Garry Tregidga, *The Liberal Party in South-West Britain since 1918: Decline, Dormancy and Rebirth* (Exeter, 2000), pp.87–96.

22. David Butler and Dennis Kavanagh, *The British General Election of 1992* (London, 1992), pp.280, 336–7.

23. David Marquand, *Ramsay MacDonald* (London, 1977), p.36; Mary Agnes Hamilton, *Arthur Henderson: A Biography* (London, 1938), p.30; Chris Wrigley, *Arthur Henderson* (Cardiff, 1990), pp.16–19.

24. *Minutes of the Rainbow Circle, 1894–1924*, Michael Freeden (ed), (London, 1989). He continued to attend occasionally even after the war, and gave a paper on 'The Labour Outlook' as late as June 1922: see ibid., pp.324–5.

25. Wrigley, *Arthur Henderson*, pp.107–8.

26. Marquand, *Ramsay MacDonald*, p.320.

27. Ibid., pp.125, 320; Wrigley, *Arthur Henderson*, pp.137–8.

28. See e.g. *The Neville Chamberlain Diary Letters, Volume 3: The Heir Apparent, 1928–33*, Robert Self (ed.), (Aldershot, 2002), p. 260, Neville to Hilda Chamberlain, 25 May 1931.

29. See Andrew Thorpe, 'J. H. Thomas and the rise of Labour in Derby, 1880–1945', *Midland History*, 15 (1990), pp.111–28.

30. See Colin Cross, *Philip Snowden* (London, 1966); Keith Laybourn, *Philip Snowden: A Biography* (Aldershot, 1988). For Snowden as a 'pensioner' see Maurice Cowling, *The Impact of Hitler: British Politics and British Policy, 1933–1940* (Cambridge, 1975), p.35.

31. Bernard Wasserstein, *Herbert Samuel: A Political Life* (Oxford, 1992), p.366; *Hugh Dalton, The Fateful Years: Memoirs 1931–1945* (London, 1957), p.200.

32. *The Second World War Diary of Hugh Dalton, 1940–45*, Ben Pimlott (ed.), (London, 1986), p.427, entry for 8 May 1942.

33. For more on this, see Michael Freeden, *Ideologies and Political Theory: A Conceptual Approach* (Oxford, 1996).

34. Freeden, *Ideologies and Political Theory*, p. 553.
35. Manchester Local Studies and Archives Service, M392/1/4, Society of Certified and Associated Liberal Agents, North West District, annual report for 1939, presented to annual meeting 16 March 1940.
36. Dorset Record Office, Dorchester, D1512/A1, East Dorset Liberal association, executive committee minutes, 29 August 1939.
37. Bodleian Library, Oxford, MSS Simon 85, folios 77–8, Sir John Simon to J. A. Spender, 10 October 1938.
38. West Yorkshire Archive Service, Bradford, 36D78/29, Bradford Liberal National association, minutes of meeting, 21 November 1938.
39. Labour Party, *Report of the Twenty-Second Annual Conference, 1922* (London, 1922), p.210.
40. Freeden, *Ideologies and Political Theory*, p.479.
41. Tanner, *Political Change and the Labour Party*, pp.44–78; A. K. Russell, *Liberal Landslide: The General Election of 1906* (Newton Abbot, 1973), pp.82–3; Neal Blewett, *The Peers. The Parties and the People: The General Elections of 1910* (London, 1972), pp.315–29, 412–15.
42. Henry Pelling, 'The politics of the Osborne judgment', *Historical Journal*, 25 (1982), pp. 889–909; McKibbin, *Evolution of the Labour Party*, pp. 20–1, 85–6. The verdict of A. J. P. Taylor, *English History 1914–1945* (Oxford, 1965), pp. 114–15, remains illuminating.
43. See e.g. G. D. H. Cole, *Self-Government in Industry* (London, 1917).
44. See e.g. University of Newcastle Library, Runciman papers, WR 221, Lord Shuttleworth to Walter Runciman, 3 December 1930.
45. Tregidga, *The Liberal Party in South-West Britain since 1918*, p.55.
46. Jose Harris, *William Beveridge: A Biography* (Oxford, 1997 edn), pp.428–32.
47. Harris, *William Beveridge*, p.432.
48. Anthony Howe, *Free Trade and Liberal England, 1846–1946* (Oxford, 1997), pp.307–8; British Library of Political and Economic Science, Beveridge papers, VI/103, folio 49, Elliott Dodds to Sir William Beveridge, 28 January 1945. This facet of wartime Liberalism is largely ignored in the otherwise excellent Richard Cockett, *Thinking the Unthinkable: Think Tanks and the Economic Counter-Revolution, 1931–1983* (London, 1994).
49. Waltham Forest Archives and Local Studies Library, uncatalogued, Walthamstow Liberal and Radical association, joint executive committee, 9 September 1939; joint officers' meeting, 9 January 1940. For example, he addressed a meeting of the local Old Age Pensions League on behalf of the local Liberal association in early 1940. He moved to York in 1940 or 1941; only then did he sever his links with the Walthamstow Liberals: ibid., joint executive committee, 10 July 1941.
50. Pelling, 'The politics of the Osborne judgment'; McKibbin, *Evolution of the Labour Party*, pp.20–1, 85–6.
51. On this see C. J. Wrigley, *Lloyd George and the Challenge of Labour: The Post-War Coalition, 1918–1922* (London, 1990).
52. Campbell, *Lloyd George: The Goat in the Wilderness*, pp.136–56.

53. Keith Middlemas and John Barnes, *Baldwin: A Biography* (London, 1969), p.412; Sir John Simon, *Three Speeches on the General Strike* (London, 1926); Thomas Jones, *Whitehall Diary*, ed. Keith Middlemas (3 vols, 1969), pp.44–5, entries for 9 and 10 May 1926.

54. University of Warwick, Modern Records Centre, Transport and General Workers' Union papers, MSS 126/T&G/1/1/7, general secretary's quarterly report, 27 May 1930; Thorpe, *British General Election of 1931*, p.56.

55. Thorpe, *British General Election of 1931*, p.121.

56. Gerard J. de Groot, *Liberal Crusader: The Life of Sir Archibald Sinclair* (London, 1993), pp.132–50.

57. Keith Laybourn and Jack Reynolds, *Liberalism and the Rise of Labour 1890–1918* (London, 1984), especially p.205.

58. For the election in Huddersfield, see the following collections in the West Yorkshire Archives Service, Kirklees (Huddersfield): Huddersfield Liberal association [Liberal Nationals]; Huddersfield borough Liberal association [Liberals]; Sir William Mabane papers.

59. Chris Cook, 'Liberals, Labour and local elections', in Gillian Peele and Chris Cook (eds), *The Politics of Reappraisal, 1918–1939* (London, 1975), pp.166–88, at pp.178–9, 186–7. Sam Davies and Bob Morley, *County Borough Elections in England and Wales, 1919–1938: A Comparative Analysis, Volume 2— Bradford–Carlisle* (Aldershot, 2000), pp.199–205; Helen Mathers, 'The City of Sheffield 1893–1926', and Andrew Thorpe, 'The consolidation of a Labour stronghold, 1926–1951' in Clyde Binfield et al. (eds), *The History of the City of Sheffield, 1843–1993* (Sheffield, 3 vols, 1993), pp.53–83, 85–118, at 58, 75–7, 85–94, 98, 117.

60. For an excellent analysis of Labour's eventual similarities with the European parties, see Stefan Berger, *The British Labour Party and the German Social Democrats, 1900–1931: A Comparative Study* (Oxford, 1994), especially pp.248–55.

61. Roy Douglas, *The History of the Liberal Party 1895–1970* (London, 1971), p.90.

62. Jeremy Thorpe, 'Foreword' in Douglas, *History of the Liberal Party*, p. xii.

63. Tanner, *Political Change and the Labour Party*, pp.21–2; Frank Bealey and Henry Pelling, *Labour and Politics 1900–1906: The History of the Labour Representation Committee* (London, 1958), pp.125–59.

64. Laybourn, *Philip Snowden*, pp.79–81; R. E. Dowse, *Left in the Centre: The Independent Labour Party 1893–1940* (London, 1966), p.43.

65. See Cline, *Recruits to Labour, passim*.

66. Thorpe, *British General Election of 1931*, p.182.

67. Blaazer, *The Popular Front and the Progressive Tradition*, p.188.

68. Michael Freeden, *Liberalism Divided: A Study in British Political Thought, 1914–1939* (Oxford, 1986), pp.177–222.

69. Ben Pimlott, *Labour and the Left in the 1930s* (Cambridge, 1977), pp.170–82.

70. Blaazer, *The Popular Front and the Progressive Tradition, passim*.

Socialist Intellectual as Social Engineer

Jan Tinbergen's ideas on economic policy and the optimal economic order (1930–60)*

Aad Blok

The transformation of northwestern European social democracy from a reformist workers' movement into a social reform movement with predominantly workers' support can generally be situated in the interwar period. After the short revolutionary wave at the end of the First World War, reformism had again established itself firmly by the early 1920s as the dominant ideological current within the social-democratic parties in northwestern Europe. By the end of the First World War, reformism had succeeded in gaining a primary political objective: universal (or at least universal male) suffrage, which would give social-democratic parties, so they expected, the parliamentary power to bring about reforms. Effective parliamentary government participation was achieved in a number of European countries, most notably of course in Weimar Germany. Based theoretically mainly on Bernstein revisionism, the reformists were convinced, with regard to political economy, that the gradual improvement of conditions for industrial organised workers through a combination of parliamentary action and trade-union organising, together with a tendency within the capitalist economy towards concentration and rationalisation, would inevitably lead to a socialist society in the longer run.[1]

The global economic crisis beginning in 1929 put an end to these reformist convictions and posed a dilemma for the social-democratic parties throughout western European countries. The reformist programme had no solutions to offer for the rapidly deepening economic crisis and the accompanying deterioration of conditions and standard of living for the working class as a result of mass unemployment and large-scale wage cuts. Politically, the reformist social-democratic parties faced growing competition from radical parties on both the left (revolutionary socialists and communists) and the extreme right (fascists and national socialists). With respect to economic theory, the reformists had based themselves predominantly on the classical Austrian school of economics, an economic theory incapable of providing an effective policy to solve the severe problems of the time. Economists from various sides, social democrats as well as others, started suggesting various degrees of counter-cyclical economic intervention by the state, Keynes of course being the most influential. At the same time, economists of various ilk showed a growing interest in forms and degrees of economic planning as a way to control the cyclical and chaotic nature of capitalist economy.[2]

Among social democrats in a number of smaller European countries, especially in Belgium and the Netherlands, the ideas of the Belgian Hendrik de Man became very influential. Based on a theoretical and ideological foundation which was explicitly intended to go beyond Marxism, he advocated the development of a 'Labour Plan' which would, among other things, regulate production by what was called 'socialisation of the power of control (over production)', create employment through large-scale public works, and implement an active economic policy that included deficit spending and a close control of business cycles. Plan-socialism, or Planism as it came to be labelled, rapidly became an important current within the social-democratic movement from the early 1930s—especially in Belgium, the Netherlands and Switzerland, where 'Labour Plans' were developed by the social-democratic parties.[3]

The actual political success of Planism before the Second World War remained very limited, but a counter-cyclical and state-interventionist economic policy to ensure social security did prove very successful during and after the Second World War, in the form of what became labelled as social Keynesianism. As Marcel van der Linden notes, Keynesianism offered social democracy important advantages. First, it allowed control over the economy via the state from above: by managing the unemployment rate and the income distribution without affecting private ownership of the means of production, a reconciliation between socialism and the market, and between entrepreneurs and workers, became possible. At the same time, Keynesianism showed that increasing consumption among broad segments of the population could stimulate economic growth, and thus provided an economic justification for a more egalitarian outlook on society. This economic growth also enabled governments to spend part of the social product on expanding social services without disrupting the economic balance.[4] Although it took a bit longer for social Keynesianism to be explicitly acknowledged by most European social-democratic parties as their ideology, it was adopted as economic policy by a growing number of northern European countries from the mid 1930s onward.[5] Moreover, the economic policy in Roosevelt's New Deal as well as in Nazi Germany offer some obvious resemblances to social Keynesianism.[6]

Intellectuals and social Keynesianism

The development of social Keynesianism into the dominant paradigm of economic policy followed a variety of trajectories in the various Western European social-democratic parties.

In this development, intellectuals from various nationalities have played a pivotal role. These included dedicated social democrats as well as social liberals, such as Keynes himself and John Kenneth Galbraith. Obviously, the leading part among these intellectuals was played by economists: developments in economics were a central precondition for the formulation and realisation of Keynesian economic policy and, thus, for the programme of social Keynesianism.[7]

Among them, the Dutch economist Jan Tinbergen (1903–94) takes a prominent position, both nationally and internationally. Tinbergen is undoubtedly the most famous economist to hail from the Netherlands. He was one of the founding fathers of econometrics, pioneer of the theory of macro-economic modelling and the theory of economic policy in a mixed economy, co-winner of the first Nobel prize for economics (in 1969, together with his Norwegian colleague Ragnar Frisch), and for many years the most cited Dutch economist. Tinbergen was not only highly esteemed among his colleagues, but also known to the public, both nationally and internationally, as a tireless advocate for a more equal and fair distribution of wealth between the First and the Third World.

Tinbergen was also a lifelong social democrat. From the 1930s he became increasingly influential within Dutch social democracy as the leading expert in the field of economic policy and economic order. As the author of numerous publications in the social-democratic press, and as intellectual originator of the Dutch Labour Plan, he can be described as the main theorist, or ideologue, of the specifically Dutch variant of pre-war Planism. Through his work on macro-economic modelling for the League of Nations, he also became a leading theorist of international stature on counter-cyclical and state-interventionist economic policy, even more so through his famous debate with Keynes on the value of statistical testing of business-cycle theories. After the Second World War he became, as architect and first director of the Dutch Central Planning Bureau, the Dutch government's main advisor on economic policy. In this capacity he helped to shape the Dutch postwar welfare state, by putting into practice the theory of economy policy he himself had developed, and which he taught, as professor at the Netherlands School of Economics in Rotterdam, to generations of economists.

In this article, I will sketch the origins and development of Tinbergen's thoughts on economic policy, economic order and social engineering in the context of Dutch and international social-democratic ideology in the period 1930–50. Subsequently I analyse to what extent his ideas have affected the Dutch and international social-democratic ideology of the period. I will try to show that Tinbergen's ideas on the optimal economic order, on the role of economics in engineering social change and in achieving this optimal order, and his view on the role of the state in the economy have been among the fundamental building blocks of the ideology of social Keynesianism and, therefore, of postwar social-democratic ideology.

In the concluding section, I will put Tinbergen and his development as a *socialist* intellectual into the broader perspective of the relationship between intellectuals and the socialist movement. In recent social theory and historiography, this relationship has been given renewed attention: the work by Radhika Desai on the history of social-democratic intellectuals in the British Labour Party and the roots of the Labour-SDP split, and Ron Eyerman's insightful study of the modern intellectual as historical category will serve here as useful sources of reference.[8] In this way, I aim to analyse first, to what extent Tinbergen can be categorised as a typical socialist 'expert-intellectual', and secondly, how his use of a socialist-inspired concept of rationality, and of the mathematical methods and language of current, positivist science enabled him to carve out a particular influential position for the modern economist as expert advisor to the state.[9]

The path towards econometrics

Tinbergen was born in 1903 into an intellectual professional *milieu*: both his parents were trained teachers. His parents were members of the Remonstrant Church—a small protestant denomination, which counted a large number of intellectuals and professionals among its membership. Albert Jolink, Tinbergen's biographer, describes the Tinbergen family as socially concerned, and although his parents were not politically active themselves, it seems Jan learned commitment to social issues at his mother's knee.[10] During his high-school years, the atrocities of the First World War, as well as the promise of a better society that the Russian Revolution seemed to carry, left a lasting impression on him, and like many of his generation, he was drawn to the socialist movement. At the age of nineteen, he joined the Dutch social-democratic Party, the SDAP.

At an early age, his extraordinary talents for mathematics and physics had become apparent, making physics the obvious choice for an academic study.

He studied physics in Leiden with the famous theoretical physicist Paul Ehrenfest, who quickly noticed Tinbergen's talents, and invited him to become one of his assistants. Meanwhile, Tinbergen became active in the social-democratic student movement SDSC, as editor of and regular contributor to its periodical *Kentering*. He also contributed to educational and vocational training programmes of the *Arbeider Jeugd Centrale* (the SDAP youth organisation), and of the *Leidse Volkshuis* (People's Home), an initiative of the local Toynbee movement.[11]

While Tinbergen's choice to study physics was a logical step given his extraordinary talent in mathematics and physics, it must soon have become clear to him that physics was not the field in which a young socialist intellectual could most effectively put his commitment to social issues into practice. Ehrenfest seems to have been a major and dual influence on Tinbergen in this respect: first, in the particularly rigorous approach to scientific training he offered his student. As Marcel Boumans has shown, Tinbergen took from his training as a physicist especially the application of mathematics as derived from classical mechanics, in which not so much the technical details but the essence of the mathematical argumentation counted.[12] But in Tinbergen's adoption of economics as the field where scientific training and knowledge could best be put into practice for the benefit of society, Ehrenfest and his wife also seem to have played a major role.

Ideologically, Tinbergen was, like many of his generation of social-democratic students, strongly influenced by Hendrik De Man who, from the early 1920s, introduced a fundamental revision of Marxism. According to De Man, the ethical motive, not the economic one, was the prime argument for the working class and for progressive intellectuals to turn to socialism.[13] This ethical motive, the conviction that social inequality needed to be opposed and solved, was predominant in Tinbergen's views on socialism and economy from his earliest writings onward. To what extent this ethical motive found its origins in his religious background (he remained a member of the Remonstrant Church throughout his life) is hard to establish. Although a parallel with religious socialism seems obvious, it is important to note that Tinbergen never explicitly or intentionally associated himself with this current in Dutch socialism, which he apparently found too anti-rational and free-floating.[14]

As a convinced pacifist, Tinbergen had conscientious objections against military service and, after finishing his physics studies in 1925, he refused to be drafted. As a result of the newly introduced Draft Resisters Act, he was, through the intervention of his father, eventually put to work at the Central Bureau for Statistics (CBS) to fulfil his alternative national service. At the CBS, he would work with the recently created department for business cycle research—with hindsight, a decisive step in his career. Combining his scientific training as physicist and mathematician, as well as his own interest and study in economics, with the statistical work on business cycles within the CBS, he laid the groundwork for his development into the main theorist of a new field: economic policy based on macroeconomic modelling. At the same time, he would become one of the founders of the new discipline of econometrics. Tinbergen obtained his PhD in 1929 with his dissertation *Minimumproblemen in de natuurkunde en de ekonomie* (Minimum problems in physics and economics), in which he showed the analogy between a number of economic and physics problems. While rounding off his training as physicist, he took his initial steps in economics. In 1929, he obtained a regular position at the CBS, which he would keep until 1946. He started lecturing in mathematical statistics at the University of Amsterdam in 1931. Two years later he was appointed extraordinary professor in statistics at the Netherlands School of Economics in Rotterdam.

During his alternative service, Tinbergen self-consciously explored his possible role as intellectual in the social-democratic movement. In a 1926 letter to F. Wibaut, one of the leading social-democratic politicians and ideologues at the time, he asked: 'What type of useful work can someone, who has had an economic-statistical training, do for the socialist movement?' He indicated that he had switched from physics to economics and statistics 'because of the conviction that the process of socialisation...is in need of forces trained in economics for every further step'.[15] His talents for the social-democratic cause were thus easily scouted by one of the leading intellectuals of Dutch social democracy between the wars. From 1928 onward, Tinbergen published regularly on economics and socialist theory in the SDAP's main theoretical journal, *De Socialistische Gids*, soon joining its editorial board in 1929.[16]

His first contributions discussed the economic theory underlying the reformist mainstream within Dutch and international social democracy. In contrast to the reformists who viewed the processes of cartelisation and rationalisation to be, in principle, a positive development from a socialist perspective, Tinbergen was rather negative about these processes. Criticising the economic theory of the reformists, he argued that a much more mathematical foundation of economic theory was needed. According to Tinbergen, real competitive capitalism had already ceased to exist since the First World War, due to processes of concentration and monopolisation, economic empowerment of organisations, both of workers—trade unions —and of employers, and the beginnings of social welfare policies by the state. All these developments had put an end to the real free working of the mechanism of supply and demand. These developments, however, could only work in the direction of a more socialist society if the state could actively control and direct economic policy through regulation. If not controlled and regulated by the state, these processes would only lead to a growing unfairness and inequality in society. The main task for the social-democratic movement, argued Tinbergen, was therefore to develop 'regulating principles', based on *ethical* considerations of social justice, to be applied by the state. The interventionist, regulating state became a central element in Tinbergen's thought. This intervention should also include wage base determination. Tinbergen deemed the trade unions' struggle for higher wages more negative than usual in mainstream social democracy: higher wages, in his view, induced employers to reduce the costs of labour, which in turn led to an uncontrolled process of rationalisation. This resulted in a high structural unemployment from the early 1920s.

When around 1930 unemployment started to rise rapidly and the economy stagnated in the severe recession commonly known as the Great Depression, the theoretical and ideological developments within the SDAP accelerated. Whereas the reformist mainstream had no other solution to offer than fighting wage cuts to maintain the working class's purchasing power, Tinbergen argued that social democracy should consider the economy-wide effects of its strategy. His ideas about regulating principles evolved into the concept of economic planning, which should then be a central instrument in social-democratic economic policy, to be realised in an economic order where the ownership of the means of production, at least in the first instance, remained unchanged.

In 1933, the reformist mainstream was more and more forced onto the defensive, due to the dramatic developments in Germany, the rise of fascism in the Netherlands, internal conflicts in the Dutch party, and the deepening of the economic crisis. In this climate, Tinbergen's ideas on economic planning and an active interventionist economic policy with deficit spending could gain momentum within the party; they were endorsed by a growing number of the younger generation in particular. Following the Belgian example, the party leadership decided in 1934 to have a Dutch Labour Plan drawn up. It contained as main elements a shorter-term policy of public works to create employment, in combination with a longer-term aim to achieve social security for everyone at a reasonable standard of living through a policy of economic planning and regulation of private enterprise in order to smooth business cycles.

When one compares the Dutch Labour Plan with Tinbergen's many publications in the early 1930s, it becomes clear how much he had prepared the ground for a specifically Dutch version of Planism. Nonetheless, Tinbergen's biographer, Albert Jolink, has recently raised doubts about the extent to which Tinbergen actively participated in the actual preparation and formulation of the Dutch Plan. First, working as a civil servant at the CBS, the possibilities for him overtly to deploy political activities for the oppositional social-democratic party were probably limited. But second, Tinbergen's orientation was more international than that of most of the mainstream social-democratic leadership at the time. In the late 1920s he started publishing in international academic journals in economics and came into contact with a growing number of economists working with newly developed concepts of economic modelling and planning. From 1931 onwards he and Wibaut were involved with an international network of planists under the umbrella of the International Industrial Relations Association/International Industrial Relations Institute (IIRA/IIRI). The explicitly *national* character of the Dutch Plan was therefore an element to which Tinbergen probably objected most: his own views on economic planning were much more internationally oriented than the formulations in the Dutch Labour Plan.[17] Nevertheless, the Dutch Plan clearly bears the marks of Tinbergen in the economic-theoretical basis in which it was grounded, and, furthermore, in the extensive statistical foundations of the argumentation.

His close friend Hein Vos was the main author of the Plan, and it is through their co-operation that state-of-the-art economic ideas and theories could become applied in a plea for an active state-interventionist, counter-cyclical economic policy. The basic assumption both of the Dutch Plan and of Tinbergen's more internationalist Planism was that an economic policy to solve the present economic crisis and mass unemployment was possible without drastically changing the economic order in the sense of who owned the means of production; only a (part) socialisation of the power of control over production, through economic regulation by the state, would be needed.

With the breakthrough of Planism, the original pursuit of socialisation leading eventually to a completely socialised economy, and thus to a socialist society, was put into a radically different perspective. Planism had closed the gap that existed in the 'old' reformist ideology between theory and practice by focussing entirely on short-term solutions for the present economic crisis. Ideologically, the socialist society became a much more distant, and, above all, much more vaguely defined ultimate goal. According to Tinbergen in 1934, the precise form of such a socialised society could well be subject to various fundamental changes along the way.[18] Whereas reformism was still based on a common Marxist conviction that in the longer run the realisation of a socialist society would be inevitable, Planism led to a blurring of such a view of future society.

The Marxist ideological framework was no longer valid for Tinbergen (if, indeed it ever had been), as for many of his generation. What can be found instead as ideological basis, is a mixture of two elements. First, there was a general ethical principle of social justice, which for Tinbergen was the principle of distributive justice. The problem of a more equal and fair distribution always took a central place in Tinbergen's thought. For him, socialism had basically become the societal system of the most equitable distribution. Second, he maintained that only through rational, scientific methods could the problems that stood in the way of this equitable distribution be analysed and solved. With Tinbergen, the primacy shifted from Marxist theory to mathematically based, quantifiable positivist science. This could be labelled as a 'scientistic' ideology: the conviction that the social could be engineered and that social change can be effected by scientific means.[19] Apart from the faith Tinbergen put in science to achieve socialist goals, he relied heavily on the *state* to ensure that no special interest groups would dominate economic policy and organisation. In this, he remained firmly in the 'statist' tradition of the previous generation of Dutch reformists.[20]

From Planism to a mixed economy and a fair distribution

Publication of the Dutch Labour Plan almost immediately established Planism as the leading ideological current within the SDAP. The ethical foundations of Planism ran parallel with religious socialism, which became increasingly influential within the SDAP in the person of Willem Banning, who became one of the leading ideologues around the mid 1930s. The departure from the classical reformist-Marxist ideological foundations found its political realisation in the ambition to reform the SDAP into a more broadly based progressive popular party, which would appeal to a larger and socially more diverse constituency. This *doorbraak* (breakthrough) materialised after the Second World War through the foundation of a new social-democratic party: the *Partij van de Arbeid*. Tinbergen became one of the main ideologues of the new party, which would play a critical role in the postwar reconstruction of the Dutch economy.

After the publication of the Dutch Labour Plan, Tinbergen had devoted himself predominantly to his scientific work, in particular to the development of dynamic macro-economic models and their practical application for an active economic policy. In 1936, he presented the first dynamic macro-economic model for the Dutch economy, consisting of a system of mathematical equations, of which the coefficients had been estimated with advanced mathematical-statistical techniques. The model could be used to trace the effects of various economic policy measures; thus, empirical testing of what would be the most desirable economic policy became possible.[21] Tinbergen's interest in the development of these macro-economic models was clearly not of a purely scientific nature; he was primarily interested in the application of dynamic modelling to ensure that the best economic policy measures could be objectively and scientifically determined.

A clear connection can thus be seen between Tinbergen's work on dynamic macro-economic modelling and the state-interventionist economic policy as promoted in Planism. Central to the planist ideas of economic policy was active state interference with the economic process, within the existing framework of the capitalist economic order. The ability to analyse the economic process as precisely as possible would be essential for such an economic policy, so as to determine when, where and how the state could best intervene. Tinbergen's macro-economic modelling provided the instruments for such an analysis.

His work on macro-economic modelling was soon internationally noticed; by then Tinbergen had already built an extensive international network amongst mathematical economists, statisticians and business cycle analysts. This led, *inter alia*, to his work for the League of Nations: in the period 1936–1938 he carried out extensive statistical and theoretical research to test existing business cycle theories. This work confirmed Tinbergen's international reputation, even more so when it was reviewed by Keynes, which led to the famous Keynes-Tinbergen controversy over the value of advanced mathematical-statistical methods in economics.[22] In this debate, Keynes questioned the validity of Tinbergen's advanced statistical methodology to test economic theory.

With Tinbergen's main attention directed toward the development of the theory of macro-economic modelling and the related mathematical-statistical methodology, less time and attention seemed to be left for involvement in social-democratic theory or politics. From his few statements on socialist theory after 1935, a gradual redirection can nevertheless be discerned in his assessment of one of the central objectives in reformist socialist theory: socialisation. In 1933, he had still called socialisation one of the leading principles of socialist theory, whereas in 1939 he seemed to have distanced himself from the idea that socialisation was one of the basic, necessary principles of socialism.[23] This redirection in Tinbergen's thought on socialist theory and the economic order was furthermore influenced by his experience of the Second World War and the German occupation of the Netherlands, which especially for Tinbergen seems to have caused an enormous rupture. As a convinced pacifist, the impact the war and Nazi occupation made on him must have been particularly strong, even more so as it was only around 1944, he later told Hein Vos, that he became convinced that Hitler could not win the war.[24] Part of the result of this impact becomes manifest in *De Les van Dertig Jaar* (The Lesson of Thirty Years) published 1944, in which he sketched his vision as economist on the desirable economic order after the war.[25] The idea of a mixed economic order takes central place in his vision of the future. Socialisation has now become for Tinbergen one of the possible means, instead of an ultimate objective. The mixed economy is no longer a transitional phase towards the socialised society, but a permanent objective. Planning, regulation, and (limited forms of) socialisation are no longer means to their own end, but instruments that can be applied to realise general economic goals.

These goals are, first of all, economic growth: given the extent of material damage at the end of the war, this took absolute priority in order to provide a basic standard of living for everyone. Subsequently, a more equal distribution of income and wealth, leading to more social justice, became for Tinbergen a major objective of social-democratic economic policy. The extent to which the instruments of planning, regulation and socialisation should be applied was to be determined by the measuring rod of their suitability and efficiency towards the given objectives of economic growth and greater equity.

Economic efficiency thus became for Tinbergen the dominant criterion in determining the optimal economic order and organisation of society. His attitude towards the system of free enterprise became much more positive than before the war. To achieve the objectives of social justice, cyclical stability, full employment and a fairer distribution of income and wealth, it would remain necessary to have a certain degree of control and regulation, but only to realise efficiency in an economic sense. This would, however, lead to a much more general macro-economic interference by the state than prewar Planism had in mind.

In addition to the economic considerations, there were also important political and ideological arguments at play in the assessment of which would be the most desirable economic system. Tinbergen's view was that personal freedom would be better guaranteed in a system of free enterprise than in a system of total collectivist planning. In a crucial essay in *Socialisme en Democratie* (*Socialism and Democracy*), the sequel to the main prewar theoretical social-democratic journal, tellingly entitled '*De derde weg*' ('The third way'), Tinbergen connected his arguments in favour of a mixed economy with the great value attached to personal freedom in the cultural characteristics of European democracies. 'Given the degree of economic and cultural development…neither the unboundedness of the American pioneer, nor the boundedness of the Russian state servant could bring the solution in Europe'.[26] In Western Europe, a middle course should therefore be taken between the extremes of East and West. This formed the basis of what became Tinbergen's convergence theory: the idea that a convergence between American-style capitalism and Soviet communism would be inevitable in the long run.

With this redirection in his opinion on socialisation, the desired economic order and necessary degree of planning and control, Tinbergen clearly diverged from the views of his prewar Planist companion Hein Vos. The latter became the first postwar minister of economic affairs in the short-lived Schermerhorn-Drees cabinet (1945–1946). In this period, he tried to introduce at high speed an extensive package of directive economic policy measures that contained many elements of the prewar Planist programme. Most of his efforts in this direction failed, however, due to parliamentary resistance from Christian democrats and liberals. One of his proposals which seem to be derived directly from the prewar Labour Plan was the foundation of the Central Planning Bureau. Vos asked his old companion Tinbergen to draw up a plan for such an organisation and to become its director. After some hesitation—among others because he envisaged a politically much more independent research organisation—Tinbergen agreed, and started working in September 1945 at the CPB in its formative stage.[27] A prolonged political struggle followed in the Dutch parliament (heavily coloured by strongly opposing ideological standpoints) over the objectives, role and competences of the newly formed Bureau. After a disappointing result for the newly formed *Partij van de Arbeid* in the first postwar elections in 1946, Vos was replaced as minister of economic affairs by a Christian democrat. The CPB became in the following year an advisory institute for the government's economic policy, designed to produce extensive advice on what came to be known as indicative planning. Contrary to its name, the CPB never took on the original role Vos had envisaged for the Bureau: a powerful state organisation for directive planning, regulation and control of the economic process.

The role played by Tinbergen in this debate is intriguing. The divergence between Tinbergen's and Vos's views on the desired degree of planning and control by the state and on the interpretation of the most desirable economic order never clearly came out into the open. More than forty years later, Tinbergen stated that he could not remember having explicitly discussed these differences of opinion with Vos at the time.[28] But comparing Tinbergen's publications of this period on these issues with the economic policy actually chosen and the degree of state intervention in the postwar Dutch economy, it becomes clear that it is Tinbergen's idea of a mixed economy, much more than Vos's Planism, that has been directional for Dutch social democracy in this period. Tinbergen's concept of a mixed economic order provided the major basis for a growing consensus among social-democratic, Christian democratic and liberal politicians, as well as among economists, about the most desirable business cycle policy, structural economic policy, and the necessary degree of state interference in the economy.[29] This implied global, strategic intervention by the state on a macro-economic level to achieve a number of generally accepted socio-economic objectives, through the means of indicative planning, provided by the CPB under Tinbergen's theoretical and practical guidance. The Dutch economic policy of the period should therefore be characterised as 'Tinbergenian', rather than Keynesian.

The leading social-democratic ideologue in the Netherlands of the 1950s, Joop den Uyl, concluded in 1956 that regarding the theory of the economic order, the concept of the mixed economy had become the dominant theory among Western European socialists, and that Tinbergen could be considered as one of the major originators of this theory. Under the maxim 'competition as far as possible, planning as far as necessary', the mixed economy had now become the ultimate goal of the socialist movement, instead of an intermediate stage.[30] The very conditional way in which the instrument of socialisation was phrased in the 1959 political programme of the *Partij van de Arbeid* can be seen as final confirmation of the reorientation of social-democratic economic theory in a 'Tinbergenian' direction.

From the mid-1950s Tinbergen became influential in yet another field of social-democratic theoretical development. As the economic order of the mixed economy proved successful to the extent that in most Western European nation states a basic level of social security for everyone could be established, and the goal of full employment was achieved in the burgeoning modern welfare state, the social-democratic theorist started looking for new horizons. A more equal and fair distribution of income and wealth, and a greater equality of opportunities through educational reforms became new issues. From the late 1940s, Tinbergen made important contributions to this new field in the theory of socialism in the modern welfare state.[31]

Socialist expert-intellectual as social engineer

Implicit in the use of a biographical perspective to analyse the influence of one person on the theoretical and ideological development of a whole political and social movement is the danger of overrating. But taking this bias into account, I would argue that an important pioneering role should be ascribed to Jan Tinbergen in the development of social-democratic theory and ideology. Both in the transition from reformist-Marxist socialism to Planism, and in the conversion of Planism into a social-democratic ideology of the mixed economy and the modern welfare state, Tinbergen's contributions to the debates have proved directional for Dutch social democracy.

Moreover, through extensive international networks of fellow economists and econometrists, planists, and social-democratic intellectuals in general, his influence is also clearly discernible at an international level, both on the development of the theory of economic policy in mixed economy, and on the development of the idea of the social responsibility, if not mission, of *engagé* economists. The best support for this last observation can be found in the recent fierce criticism on the 'Tinbergenian' concept of social engineering from economist Deidre McCloskey in her recent *The Vices of Economists* (1996). For McCloskey, who acknowledges Tinbergen as one of the genuine world figures in modern economics, he is the original representative of the most fundamental vice of modern economics: the illusion of social engineering.[32]

When we move from the individual biographical level to the broader perspective of the relationship between intellectuals and the socialist movement to look at the position of the intellectual from a sociological or social theory perspective, the Gramscian distinction between the traditional and organic intellectual is an obvious staring point. Taking Gramsci as her point of departure, Radhika Desai analyses the position of British intellectuals as typical traditional intellectuals who by the absence of an intellectually favourable culture among conservatives were more or less automatically drawn to the Left, resulting in a historical context where 'the principal intellectual tradition tended to be progressive and critical, but not radically oppositional. Historically it functioned to incorporate the working class into the existing political system.' There are striking similarities between Tinbergen's development into a social-democratic intellectual and the story, as told by Desai, of a number of British intellectuals who were drawn to the Labour Party in the interwar years.[33] The figure of Hugh Dalton in particular makes an interesting comparison. Just like Tinbergen's position in the

Dutch social-democratic party, Dalton's role as a central intellectual influence on the Labour Party stretches out from the early 1930s across the Second World War.[34] It was Dalton, together with one of his pupils, Douglas Jay, who adapted Keynes' macro-economic ideas for an anti-employment strategy for neo-socialist, planist purposes, in a way that was very similar to Tinbergen's influence on the Dutch Labour Plan.[35]

Another interesting comparison can be made between Tinbergen's career as a socialist intellectual and the trajectory of a typical expert-intellectual from Norway: Ragnar Frisch, Tinbergen's 'comrade in arms' in the establishment of econometrics as new paradigm in economics. Besides his academic work in the development of econometrics, he was active as an economic advisor for the Norwegian Labour Party from the 1930s. In this capacity he explored how rigorous restructuring of the economy, as proposed by the Norwegian Labour Party in their Crisis Programme of 1934, should be financed, and played an important advisory role in the development of the system of administrative planning that was introduced in Norway after 1945.[36]

A more theoretically informed comparison can be made, to conclude, if we turn to the work of Ron Eyerman. To analyse the emergence of the modern intellectual as a distinct historical category Eyerman develops a theoretical framework in which tradition, role and context are interrelated in a dynamic process. By describing four prototypical intellectuals in their respective historical and cultural contexts, he shows how they draw upon existing traditions in the process of constructing a new intellectual role, that of the expert intellectual. Sketching the respective careers of John Maynard Keynes in Britain, Walter Lippmann in the United States, and Gunnar and Alva Myrdal in Sweden, Eyerman concludes that they were 'instrumental in constructing a new intellectual role, the academic expert, based on a new relationship between the intellectual and the state…Many other examples could have been called upon, as this intellectual role has become central to the functioning of modern society and to our understanding of the term *intellectual* itself.'[37] The case of Gunnar and Alva Myrdal, in particular, offers striking similarities with Tinbergen's trajectory in this regard. Like Tinbergen, the Myrdals joined the social-democratic party early in their careers and participated in both internal policy debates and in public discussions on the basis of their academic expertise on economics and social sciences, deriving their arguments from a rational, scientific world view. Both the Myrdals and Tinbergen played a pivotal role, in their respective contexts of national social-democratic politics and culture, in bringing about a paradigmatic shift in social-democratic policy and ideology.[38]

The analysis given in this article of Tinbergen's career as socialist intellectual and his development into expert advisor on economic policy shows that not only could he serve well as another example of the new intellectual role Eyerman has defined, but that Tinbergen is archetypal for a specific version of this role: the social-democratic expert-intellectual as social engineer.

Notes

* I would like to thank Marcel van der Linden for his advice and encouragement to take up this theme once more, also Jesse Vorst for his expert comments on an earlier draft and for his valuable editorial advice.

1. Marcel van der Linden, 'Metamorphoses of social democracy', in: idem, *Transnational Labour History: Explorations* (Aldershot, 2003), pp.97–8; Donald Sassoon, *One Hundred Years of Socialism: the West European left in the twentieth century* (London and New York, 1996), ch.2.
2. Sassoon, *One Hundred Years*, pp.60–9.
3. D. Pels, 'Hendrik de Man and the Ideology of Planism', *International Review of Social History*, 32 (1987), pp.206–29; Erik Hansen, 'Depression decade crisis: social democracy and planisme in Belgium and the Netherlands, 1929–1939', *Journal of Contemporary History*, 16 (1981), pp.293–322; Peter Dodge, *Beyond Marxism: the faith and works of Hendrik de Man* (The Hague, 1966).
4. Van der Linden, 'Metamorphoses', p.99.
5. Margaret Weir and Theda Skocpol, 'State structures and social Keynesianism: responses to the Great Depression in Sweden and the United States', *International Journal of Comparative Sociology*, 24 (1–2) (1983), pp.4–29.
6. Van der Linden, 'Metamorphoses', pp.98–9, and n.23.
7. Van der Linden, 'Metamorphoses', p.98; Sassoon, *One Hundred Years*, pp.60–9; C.G. Uhr, 'Economists and policymaking 1930–1936: Sweden's experience', *History of Political Economy*, 83 (1977), pp.89–121; George Garvy, 'Keynes and the economic activists of pre-Hitler Germany', *Journal of Political Economy*, 83 (1975), pp.391–405.
8. Radhika Desai, *Intellectuals and Socialism: 'Social Democrats' and the British Labour Party* (London, 1994); Ron Eyerman, *Between Culture and Politics. Intellectuals in modern society* (Cambridge, 1994). For an interesting use of Eyerman's work on the modern intellectual, see Terry Irving and Sean Scalmer, 'Australian Labour Intellectuals: an Introduction', *Labour History*, 77 (November, 1999), pp.1–10; and idem, 'Labour Intellectuals in Australia: Modes, Traditions, Generations, Transformations', *International Review of Social History*, 50 (2005), pp.1–27.
9. The term 'expert-intellectual' and the closely related term 'academic-intellectual' in Eyerman, *Between Culture and Politics*, ch.5.
10. More extensive biographical information on Tinbergen can be found in Albert Jolink, *Jan Tinbergen: The Statistical Turn in Economics, 1903–1955* (Rotterdam,

2003), ch.2, and idem, 'Jan Tinbergen', in: J. van Daal and A. Heertje (eds), *Economic Thought in the Netherlands, 1650–1950* (Aldershot, 1994), pp.183–206.

11. Jolink, *Jan Tinbergen*, pp.19–23.

12. For the historical development of Tinbergen's mathematical method and an analysis of the roots of this method in Ehrenfest's theoretical physics, see Marcel Boumans, *A Case of Limited Physics Transfer. Jan Tinbergen's resources for reshaping economics* (Amsterdam, 1992).

13. D. Pels, 'Hendrik de Man en *De Psychologie van het Socialisme*. Een samenvatting voor de jaren tachtig', in: Jan Bank (ed.), *Het vijfde jaarboek voor het democratisch socialisme* (Amsterdam 1984), pp.90ff.

14. Letter to author from H. Verwey-Jonker, 4 November 1987.

15. Cited in Jolink, *Jan Tinbergen*, p.32. Translation of original citation by Jolink.

16. J. Tinbergen, 'Opmerkingen over ruiltheorie', *De Socialistische Gids*, 1928, I, pp.431–45, deel II, pp.539–48.

17. Jolink, *Jan Tinbergen*, pp.107–19.

18. J. Tinbergen, 'Socialisme', in: *Waar gaan wij heen? Kapitalisme, socialisme, communisme, fascisme* (Amsterdam, n.d. but 1934), p.100.

19. This characteristic in M.H.J. Dullaart, *Regeling of vrijheid. Nederlands economisch denken tussen de wereldoorlogen* (Alblasserddam, 1984), p.274. Cf. J.A.A. van Doorn, 'Corporatisme en technocratie. Een verwaarloosde polariteit in de Nederlandse politiek', *Beleid en Maatschappij* (1981), pp.134–50, who points out the strong tradition of Saint-Simonism within Dutch social democracy.

20. M.H.J. Dullaart, 'The embarrassment of freedom', in: van Daal and Heertje (eds), *Economic Thought*, pp.183–206.

21. On the mathematical roots of Tinbergen's method in this respect, see Boumans, *Case of Limited Physics Transfer*.

22. Jolink, *Jan Tinbergen*, pp.170–206.

23. J. Tinbergen, *De Konjunktuur*, p.181; Tinbergen's foreword in Ed. van Cleeff, *Sociaal-economische Ordening. Een ideologisch-sociologische beschouwing uit religieus standpunt* (Arnhem, 1939).

24. Hein Vos, 'De Nobelprijs voor Tinbergen', *Socialisme en Democratie*, 26 (1969), p.503.

25. J. Tinbergen, *De les van dertig jaar. Economische ervaringen en mogelijkheden* (Amsterdam, 1944).

26. J. Tinbergen, 'De derde weg (tussen vrije en gebonden economie)' in *Socialisme en Democratie*, 3 (1946), p.371.

27. On the early history of the CPB, see Ed. van Cleeff, 'De voorgeschiedenis van het Centraal Planbureau', in *Vijfentwintig Jaar Centraal Planbureau* (The Hague, 1970), pp.7–22; Adrienne van den Bogaard, *Configuring the Economy: the emergence of a modelling practice in the Netherlands, 1920–1955* (Amsterdam, 1998).

28. Interview with Tinbergen by the author, February 1988.

29. Cf. F. ter Heide, *Ordening en verdeling. Besluitvorming over sociaal-economisch beleid 1949–1958* (Kampen, 1986), p.202. Ter Heide explains this consensus among social-democratic, Christian democratic and liberally orientated economists—

which he labels as *convergence*—by the fact that they had a common breeding ground at the Rotterdam School of Economics where Tinbergen taught as extraordinary professor from 1933.

30. Den Uyl, 'Theorie en Beweging', in: idem, *Inzicht en Uitzicht: Opstellen over economie en politiek* (Amsterdam, 1978), pp.37–43, 38.

31. His first publication on this, *Redelijke inkomensverdeling* (Reasonable Income Distribution) appeared in 1946; his most fundamental contribution to this field appeared in 1975: *Income Distribution. Analysis and policies* (Amsterdam, 1975).

32. Deidre McCloskey, *The Vices of Economists. The virtues of the bourgeoisie* (Amsterdam, 1996), pp.99–119.

33. Desai, *Intellectuals and Socialism*, pp.49–60.

34. Desai, *Intellectuals and Socialism*, pp.57–60.

35. Sassoon, *One Hundred Years*, p.62.

36. Van den Boogaard, *Configuring the Economy*, pp.78–80, 82–7.

37. Eyerman, *Between Culture and Politics*, p.160.

38. Eyerman, *Between Culture and Politics*, pp.150ff.

Donald Sassoon: History without Manifestoes

Interview by Willie Thompson

Perhaps you could start by telling us something about your academic and political background?

Well, I was born in 1946 and had the luck of growing up in a number of countries. I was at school in France and then in Italy and finally in Britain, where I did virtually everything from A level to PhD, except for the MA, which I got in the United States. Perhaps I should also add that I came to history a little bit late. My first degree was in economics which I would recommend to any historian and my second was in political science, which was in the United States. Then when I came back to Britain I wanted to do a PhD with Eric Hobsbawm and for technical reasons he advised me to register in politics on the grounds that I would never get a job with three degrees each in a different discipline. So I stuck to political science and he agreed to supervise me. As it turned out the first job I actually got was in history, much to my delight I must say. Looking back on it, it was an escape.

And where was your first job?

Westfield College, which was then a college of the University of London. It then merged with Queen Mary and it is now called just Queen Mary, University of London. So, in fact I have been employed by the University of London throughout and my first degree was at University College, London and my PhD was at Birkbeck, so one could say that really I have only known well the University of London and I am fairly ignorant about other places.

But presumably you have done a lot of academic travelling.

I have done an enormous amount of travelling, especially in the last five or six years, and I have also taught elsewhere. I taught for a while in Italy and had a visiting chair there and I was a research fellow in New York and, yes, I know some parts of the world. But I have been in London for forty years now.

How do the changes in British academia strike you over that period?
Well on the whole fairly favourably. Here I must talk about history, or at least history with social sciences, because I am obviously quite unfamiliar with science subjects. I think the improvement in history has been extraordinary over the last thirty or forty years. It is true that my generation, I should say our generation, has not produced many stars of the Edward Thompson, Eric Hobsbawm, Fernand Braudel kind of level, but nevertheless I am pretty sure that, on average, we are an awful lot better than they were thirty years ago. History has become a much wider subject. It is no longer mainly political history, with perhaps economic history as a second best, and the young generation of historians is more cultured and more widely read. It is particularly better read theoretically than its predecessors, again with the usual exceptions. I'm excluding the stars of the profession, Hobsbawm, E. P. Thompson and so on.

What was the subject of your PhD?
The Italian Communist Party, which I then published as a book here, *The Strategy of the Italian Communist Party.*

Did you have access to the PCI archives?
Not at all. The archives post-war had been in a complete mess and had only recently been put on some kind of reasonable footing so that no one, in my days doing a PhD on the post-war Italian Communist Party, had access to these archives. I must say that now that they are open and people have looked into them, nothing extraordinary has been found. Novelties about the particular behaviour of this or that leader, this or that personality, yes; but no major thesis about the Italian Communist Party has changed as a result of the opening of the archives. Those who thought that its so-called independence from Moscow was overstressed believed there would be revelations; those who, like me, thought that it was pretty independent, continue to believe that, and no one has changed their mind. It is a terrible thing to say in a journal of socialist history, but I think that archive research, particularly when one talks of the longer period, is much overrated. I am sure you disagree.

No, I actually tend to agree with you. What was the main conclusion that you reached from your study of the PCI?
Well, the PhD and also the book was an attempt to reconstruct the political line, the political strategy of the Italian Communist Party. In a sense I wanted to know the vicissitudes of its official position, which is why archives would not have helped. I was under the influence of Althusser in

those days and I wanted to treat the Italian Communist Party as a collective intellectual (the Gramscian formulation), an intellectual that produces a text. So what I did was read everything produced by the Italian Communist Party in that period, to see to what extent one could find some kind of coherence. There was a great deal of it.

I dealt with the strategy chronologically from 1944 to 1956 and then I changed tack for the years 1956–64, taking this period as a single coherent phase in which the party tried to develop a view on what kind of reforms one could have, or should have, in a capitalist society; the changes in the international context; the idea of polycentrism, which was one of Togliatti's key concepts; and also what kind of organisation the party should have. I chose the Italian Communist Party not just because I could read Italian having grown up there; equally I could have chosen the French party as French is my mother tongue. I chose the Italian communists because it seemed to me, at least in their theoretical and intellectual output, they were far more interesting than the French and this was something that everybody would agree with. Also that they were also big enough to have, or to be subject to, the constraints of a large party. Smaller communist parties in the west had fewer constraints. All parties have constraints, but obviously the smaller the party, to some extent, the main preoccupation becomes that of holding the rank and file together. Whereas, the Italian Communist Party, though in opposition, was dealing constantly with parliamentary problems, with new legislation to be amended, and of course they were running a large number of municipalities. So that was a very particular kind of communist party.

So what was your overall conclusion—or did you have one?
Not really. No. I don't think there was a headline. What was intriguing to me was the methodological aspect: how does one write the history of a party, particularly a communist party, where ideology is so important. To that extent one gives weight to a particular theoretical pronouncement. And above all what was the connection between the real world and what the party said? The most boring dispute in the historiography of the Italian Communist Party, which borrowed the name of *doppiezza*, duplicity, from a statement by Togliatti, is on the issue that the party may pretend to be democratic yet, if you scratch it, you find Stalinism. I find arguments like that particularly uninteresting because if a large party, which must appeal to an electorate and obtain mass support, says the same things over and over again, then whatever the original intention was, in the longer run, it makes no difference at all. Activists are recruited on the basis of the official line and you can't change it that easily.

One of my conclusions was that there was no question about the independence and the autonomy of the party, its commitment to democracy, to parliamentary democracy in the 'western sense'. Of course events since have abundantly confirmed this, but at the time much of the non-left historiography on communist parties was influenced by Sovietologists. They simply used their model and applied it indiscriminately to whatever party they happened to be dealing with. I remember particularly one episode when, for the sixtieth anniversary of the October revolution, Berlinguer went to Moscow and was extremely critical of the Soviet Union in a public speech, including their position on Czechoslovakia. Leonard Shapiro, the famous Sovietologist, was interviewed on the radio. He was extremely competent, of course, about the Soviet Communist Party and about the Soviet Union but when he was asked about the Italian Communist Party he simply answered, 'well, western communists speak like this for electoral purposes'. Even if true it would have made a considerable difference since Togliatti, in 1956, supported the Soviet intervention in Hungary. When eventually communism collapsed and the PCI decided to change its name, those who disagreed were only between five and ten per cent of the activists—and few of these could really be called 'Stalinists'.

What are your views on what's happened to the communist parties since the collapse of the communist world?
Well, in the west there were really few communist parties with some possibility of winning elections. Other communist parties could have no greater ambition than being a left-wing pressure group on the main social-democratic party—as in Sweden. That's a perfectly reasonable strategy. Those who did not wish to follow that strategy, like the Portuguese, failed miserably even before the communist bloc and the Soviet Union collapsed. Then you had the French and the Italian communist parties, and perhaps the Spanish. The French and the Spanish parties were in crisis before the end of the Soviet Union. The PCF in the late 1970s had become the second party of the left, and the socialists were able to dictate terms.

In France, when the left won the election in 1981 the communist party was not even necessary to form a coalition government. At that stage a large number of people, particularly workers, who had voted communist, not out of any great ideological commitment to communism but because they wanted to support the most militant left party, switched their allegiance towards a party like the socialists that could exercise real power. The numbers of activists remaining in the ranks of the PCF decreased and this would have gone on regardless of what happened in the USSR.

In the case of the Italian Communist Party we cannot really be certain about anything because the collapse of the Soviet Union coincided with the collapse of the Italian party system for reasons which had nothing to do with Gorbachev. The Italian party system collapsed because of the corruption scandals which destroyed both the Christian Democratic Party and the Italian Socialist Party, whose hope it was to do in Italy what Mitterrand had achieved in France. The reformed Communist Party (eventually called the Left Democrats) eventually absorbed some of the socialist activists and remained, not just the largest party of the left, but the second party in Italy. Would they have had more votes, more power without the collapse of the Soviet Union? It is almost impossible to say.

Do you think that changing the name and the splitting with the Refoundation Communists was the appropriate move in the circumstances?
I have been pondering about that. Obviously, the original intention was to restructure the whole of the left by eliminating a name which was an embarrassment for many people outside the Communist Party, thus creating a large party of the left which would include everybody from the far left to social democrats. This failed completely. There are more parties on the left now in Italy than ever before. What would have been the case had they kept the name? Now that is difficult to know. It would have been increasingly funny, I must say, to have in the Italy of today a party called the Communist Party. There are new generations for whom communism means Stalin, whereas for the generation in the 1960s and 1970s it almost certainly did not mean Stalin, because all Italians knew at least one or two communists, and they perfectly well knew that that they had little to do with Stalin. So probably the name would have had to be changed anyway, but certainly the great hopes of 1989 that there would be a big party of the left were completely dashed.

I take it the present outcome is the only one that could have been foreseen in the current political circumstances?
The problem with historians is that we are lumbered with the fact that we see the outcome of a series of events and that outcome seems almost inevitable, however much we try to say that nothing is inevitable and that if this and this or that had happened then something else could have happened instead. It's very difficult to trace it back. We find it very difficult to find out why the outcome is what it turned out to be, let alone trying to do a lot of counterfactual stuff!

Yes, I take your point very much. There are some historical situations, though,

in which a specific outcome is clearly overwhelmingly probable if not inevitable.
For example?

Well, by 1943 the defeat of the Third Reich.
Oh yes, but you are quite cleverly taking a conjuncture where nearly all other considerations have little play except the military/economic ones. It is like predicting the outcome of a football match when one side is left with only six players and the other has the best eleven in the world. In 1940 it was not so obvious.

OK, point taken. Do you think that the idea of the PCI's 'Historic Compromise' had anything going for it or was that an illusory strategy?
No, I think that it was one of the most brilliant strategies invented or developed by a left-wing party anywhere in Europe since 1945. At the base of the Historic Compromise was the reality that it was impossible to run Italy purely as a popular-front coalition with the socialist and communist parties. Given the character of the socialist party, subsequent to 1976, it would have been the least reliable party with whom one could have ever hoped to conclude an alliance. The second element of the Historic Compromise is that the Catholic world in Italy was a highly diversified world in which you had reactionaries and progressives and all sorts of people in between. It was not a monolithic bloc, just a large number of people held together by Catholicism but otherwise disagreeing about many things. Therefore to try to conclude an alliance with the Catholic world might have brought about the disengagement of right-wing and left-wing elements. And this is exactly what has now happened. The Christian Democratic Party has collapsed. Those on the right sided with Berlusconi and without the help of left Catholics, such as Prodi, it would be absolutely unthinkable that the left would ever return to power in Italy. The only time the left has been in power in Italy has been with Christian Democrats, or at least with Catholics.

But there is the argument though that capturing office on that basis inevitably means that nothing very fundamental is going be changed.
No, nothing fundamental is going to be changed, not because of the kind of allies the left might have in government but because of the kind of economic and political systems which exist. That is the real constraint. Any party of the left has got to face the fact that they have to run a capitalist system and therefore they have to accept all the limitations of a capitalist system integrated with that of other countries—whether the country is inside the European Union or not. So yes, had the Italian Communist Party gone into

power with the Christian Democrats, as the Historical Compromise advocated, it would not have been a revolution—obviously not—nor would they even have been able to change things in a radical fashion. Hardcore communists, like harcore leftists, would have been disappointed.

One might then ask what the point of having a communist party is?
Well the point of having a communist party is really the same as the question of what is the point of having parties on the left—which is what all people on the left have got to ask themselves. In fact, they do ask themselves and come up, repeatedly, with different answers. There are the millenarian ones, of whom there are very few left, who dream of changing society completely. And there are the more pragmatic and realistic ones who hope to use all the nooks and crannies of the existing system in order to shift resources, power and possibilities from one group of people to another group of people, which is indeed what the left has done even in opposition over the last hundred years. The vast majority of the great reforms of the last hundred years have either been conceded by the right because they were afraid of the left or else implemented by the left.

You mentioned that you were influenced by Althusser at the time that you wrote your PhD. Are you still influenced by him?
Not really, no. There was little in a practical way that one could do with Althusser, but he taught many, including myself, to take Marx seriously, in a way which I had not seen done before. For me, Althusser meant the renunciation of dogmatic marxism. It made me less dogmatic, because Althusser in his attempts to find the real Marx in the works of Marx had to decide which aspects of the works were wrong. Thus he was far from being a fundamentalist who had to accept every pronouncement as gold dust. I found that quite illuminating in the 1960s when I started reading Althusser. The concept of structure, as used by Althusser, I also found very useful as a historian. But there were also some bizarre pronouncements which one could not take seriously.

How justified do you think E. P. Thompson's onslaught on Althusser was?
I think it was bad tempered, frankly, and not conducive to anything in particular. It made him waste time instead of doing the kind of stuff he was good at.

I believe you also wrote a polemic against the New Left Review?
Well there was a new short-lived journal, called *Politics and Power* for which

I wrote a very lengthy piece called 'The Silences of New Left Review' which was mainly about the lack of interest that the *NLR* had about Britain and about British politics and also the systematic way in which they had eliminated from the canon people they did not like. *NLR* defined what European marxism was by leaving out those thinkers they did not particularly like. Afterwards—though not because of my article I am sure!—the *New Left Review* became far more engaged with British politics and British history.

Perhaps it was because of Thatcher rather than your article!
Oh, I have not the slightest illusion that they took much notice of my article. I am sure it was a complete coincidence.

How do you see the current situation in Britain?
It's in the deepest political crisis in its entire history, paradoxically in an economy which actually is doing pretty well, with unemployment fairly low. In the past Labour governments have ended up with a tiny majority, with a Conservative Party optimistic about its future while everyone thinks that they are incompetent and that the country is going to the dogs. In 1997 Labour had enormous advantages. It had a massive majority. The Conservatives were in crisis. The economy was fine, even in 1997. So all the conditions for a strong Labour government were in place then. Labour prestige in Europe was enormous. I have travelled throughout Europe and elsewhere in the last four or five years and I have been asked many times of course to speak about the left. Initially the pro-Blair attitude on the left in Germany, in France and in Italy was palpable. There was a great deal of admiration, a feeling that this was a social-democratic prime minister, leading a party with a strong majority in one of Europe's leading countries. How wonderful. Besides Labour came into power at a time when a unique conjuncture had existed: the left was in power in twelve of the then fifteen countries of the European Union including the four most important: Italy, France, and Germany and Britain. This had never happened before.

Now after so many years, those who still wish to defend the government always produce the same list, for example that poverty has been reduced—though not all statisticians agree—and devolution has been given to Scotland and Wales, though in Wales it was hardly the wish of the overwhelming majority. The list goes on but does not actually amount to much. If we look at the so-disliked Wilson governments with their reduced majorities and examine their record, in particular the civil liberties advances of the 1960s, we marvel at its courage and how much it contributed to change the country. They got rid of capital punishment and the criminalisation of homosexuals: abortion was legalised; equal pay for women was introduced. There was a long list one can be proud of. I would challenge members of the present administration to furnish a list which is of that kind of calibre. On the negative side of the balance sheet, we have an extraordinary spectacle of the Labour government being outflanked on the left by Chirac, who wanted more protection for workers in the new European constitution. The mistakes over Iraq are obvious to all except to Blair and his supporters. Even the French Mitterrand government for the first seven years introduced more reforms and improvements than Labour. The Jospin government introduced the thirty-five hour week. The Blair government cannot claim anything of that kind.

So what do you see as the most appropriate strategy for the left to adopt —that is, those of us who do not have seats in the government? What do you think we should be doing?

Well I really have no idea what you should be doing. I am not active politically and I am just a historian, you know. I will write about the past but I'm not one for having manifestoes. The European context is important. Many on the left regard Europe as its last chance, which is a paradox since the European left was originally solidly against Europe, including the German SPD and the Italian communists, of course, and not just the Labour Party. Europe had started as a conservative institution, its architecture was conservative. However, even though there are still some people on the left who are against European integration, the bulk of the opposition now comes from the right, sometimes the far right, in all the various countries.

So the battle over Europe is now clearer. The right tries to make the European economy as market-oriented as possible. The left should try to make Europe as much as possible as a political union where market regulation and the protection of labour rights prevail. The particular advantage is that, while the left finds it difficult to fight for these policies at the national level, it is easier to do so at the regional, i.e. European, level. It is difficult to convince entrepreneurs in a single country to give their workers greater wages or greater benefits than their competitors in other countries. But when legislation is enforced in the whole of the Europe region, they can no longer compete on who can squeeze their workers more. They have to find other ways of achieving profitability. Well that's obviously very good terrain for the left to fight, because in spite of all the talk about globalisation most trade is still regionally based and most trading by European countries is with other European countries. So that even at the simple reformist level the EU provides these possibilities.

The big stumbling block is the difficulty in moving towards even more centralisation. There are very few people who want that and it is very difficult to argue in favour of it. I have no problem arguing in favour of it but I am not a politician and I don't want to be elected. I can very well see that if you do want to be elected nationally, to transfer authority to a wider body, to a supranational body, is something which it is exceedingly difficult to convince others to do. So the problem is, though Europe can give the left its best hope, it is also a difficult terrain on which to fight elections and not just in Britain. It is also difficult to demand greater democratisation, when this would entail a transfer of power to more representative European bodies, because clearly the ones that we have now are not very representative.

Maybe we could look at some of the things you have written since One Hundred Years of Socialism. *Your latest book is about the Mona Lisa?*
Yes. I hate being autobiographical but here it is unavoidable. Having spent the whole of my life writing on political parties and political parties of the left, once I had finished the *Hundred Years of Socialism* I was either going to do the parties of the right or I was going to do more of the parties of the left, and at my age, and in my profession, you can't change jobs. I am stuck as a university teacher, and I like doing research, and I thought enough was enough with political parties. Reading what they write and what they do is not really terribly exciting and reading party congresses is dismal—even though, since most of the documents are written using only two hundred words or so I can understand them even in languages I don't know very well, so I could even read the Portuguese Communist Party congress in Portuguese!

I thought I would do something completely different so I have been writing a massive book which I hope I would have finished in 2005, which is a history of culture, particularly cultural markets and the cultural industry in Europe since 1800. In the course of doing this mega-work—another thousand pages of text I am afraid—I became interested in the process whereby a work belonging to high culture becomes 'pop'. Since I know a little more about music than visual art, I thought I would use as an example Beethoven's *Fifth Symphony* or Vivaldi's *Four Seasons*, something that everybody knows. I then realised that one of the conditions for wide popularity was that the artefact had to be consumed in no more than two minutes. Beethoven's *Fifth* as such is not universally known; only the first bars are, or the chorale from the *Ninth Symphony*. I concluded that the Mona Lisa was much better for an example. I started collecting facts on the Mona Lisa and the story as it began to emerge warranted more than a paragraph, it warranted more than a chapter. It turned out to be a very interesting book to write. Why a particular painting has become so famous? How was this achieved? How did it become

...iconic?

Yes, how did that happen? Real art historians do not answer that question because they are interested in the aesthetics of the thing. Someone who is not an art historian could have something to say about this. So the book is really about the nineteenth and twentieth centuries when the Mona Lisa was invented.

And what are you planning after you have finished this long book of culture, being still a very young historian!

Young? I am not far from retirement. After that book I will write a very short book, a seriously short book, on the origins of fascism in Italy and in particular on the connection between the takeover of power by Benito Mussolini and the wider conjuncture as it existed in Italy. I want to look at the micro element: why Mussolini? why not someone else? And then the wider macro question: why Italy? what was the overall context? It will be like a long essay of forty thousand words. Beyond that I don't know, but the most important thing is to finish my book on culture. This is a book no one has ever done before: it is the history of the production and consumption of culture in the whole of Europe in the nineteenth and twentieth centuries: books, newspapers, theatre, concerts, opera, variety shows, radio, the gramophone, and, of course, the cinema, television and the comic strip, etc. I want to try to see their interconnections. I now fear that the reason why no-one has done this before is that no-one was quite that stupid before. But anyway, I have had a lot of fun researching it.

Forum
New Labour in perspective

New Labour, science, and democracy

Much energy has been spent debating whether or not New Labour is new or whether or not it remains properly socialist.[1] These debates provide settings in which commentators can commend or oppose New Labour, but they have little other value. Contributors to the debates propound definitions of socialism, which exhibit different degrees of historical sophistication, before then comparing New Labour with these definitions. However, it is important to remember that ideologies are historical; they are contingent and changeable clusters of ideas; they do not possess core values or policies. The definitions of socialism by which people have sought to judge the authenticity of New Labour as a development or expression of socialism are, therefore, unable to fulfil the role ascribed to them—they cannot capture the essence of socialism, or its legitimate historical trajectory, for there is no such thing.

The debate about New Labour's relationship to the socialist tradition is often misconceived because it reifies that tradition. When we allow properly for contingent agency within history, we grant that novelty and change are inherent, ubiquitous features of human life. Political actors always confront slightly novel situations, and, because a tradition does not fix its own application, their responses to these situations are inevitably open-ended sites at which they modify and develop inherited traditions. New Labour is a novel development of socialism precisely because all political parties are perpetually remaking themselves as novel entities. The only appropriate questions are, therefore, those that concern the content, and possibly the extent, of this novelty. When historians address the different question of whether or not New Labour is new, they are being seduced by reified concepts; they make sense of the latter question by assuming, explicitly or implicitly, that New Labour might or might not have broken with a set of objectified norms, values, or policies that they mistakenly take to have been constitutive of the party.

New Labour and social science

In what ways and for what reasons has New Labour remade its socialist inheritance? How has it responded to which issues against the background of what patterns of thought? One way of approach these questions is, once again, to query the idea of a core set of socialist principles. We might start to talk instead about different, overlapping but also competing socialist traditions which can be traced through Labour's history.

If we are seeking to understand New Labour, it is especially helpful, I believe, to highlight some different concepts of democracy adopted by British socialists.[2] Liberal and Fabian socialists often argued the state had to take on new functions associated with taxation, public provision of welfare, and nationalisation; they called for an extension of democracy to ensure this more active state remained trustworthy. Others, notably non-governmental socialists and syndicalists, argued that civil society needed to be purged of abuses they associated with competitive individualism; they called for the democratisation of civil society itself. For non-governmental socialists, civil society needed to embody the democratic spirit of true fellowship. For syndicalists, many of the associations in civil society needed to be made thoroughly democratic. Socialists spent much time, then, debating the relative roles of a democratic state and democratic associations in civil society. To simplify, we might say that the dominant tradition fused liberal socialism and Keynesian economics to emphasise the role of the state, but it was opposed by socialists influenced by non-governmental themes in ethical socialism and Marxism.

New Labour represents a liberal socialist response to the New Right. It follows liberal socialism in privileging representative democracy as the context within which experts then can formulate and implement policies to solve social problems. And it often appears to be preoccupied by that the New Right brought to the fore of political debate, problems such as inflation and the underclass. Although New Labour is often responding to issues associated with the New Right, typically it does not conceive of these problems in terms of the monetarism and public choice theory of the New Right. New Labour's preferred forms of social science are the new institutionalism and communitarianism. One reason New Labour has been attracted to these social sciences is their use of a social concept of the self as the basis for a critique of public choice and neoliberalism. They chime with New Labour's attempts to reassert a socialist tradition against what it condemns as the excessive individualism of Thatcherism. New Labour draws on communitarianism to argue that Thatcherite individualism exasperated social fragmentation; only recognition of our social nature and responsibilities can sustain a healthy society. And it draws on the new institutionalism to argue that the Thatcherite enthusiasm for markets led to a short termism that mitigated against the investment, innovation, and collaboration needed in the new hi-tech global economy; only the promotion of networks and partnerships can led to long-term economic vitality and prosperity. Equally, the institutionalism and communitarianism provided New Labour with resources with which to distance itself from Old Labour thereby forestalling some of the aspects of Conservative criticism of the party's past that so resonated with voters. Old Labour is accused, as communitarianism suggests, of promoting a rights-based culture that neglects individual responsibility. And it is associated, as new institutionalism suggests, with inflexible hierarchies rather than the networks and partnerships allegedly required to meet the demands of the new economy.

The expertise of the new institutionalists and communitarians pervades New Labour's ideas. The Blair governments have followed the new institutionalism in promoting networks and partnerships as the primary structures by which to deliver services. And they have followed communitarianism in attempting to reform the welfare state so as to foreground personal responsibility within the settings of family and work. The broad contours of New Labour's policies often derive from these ideas from social science. Its welfare reforms have tried to transform the role of the state into that of an enabling partner concerned to promote responsibility as well as to guarantee rights; they have encouraged a broad shift toward joined-up governance and networks as modes of service delivery. Likewise, its economic policies have combined a focus on macro-economic stability with efforts to revitalise the supply-side of the economy through the government involvement in training and networks. New Labour draws heavily, I am arguing, on communitarianism, with its moralistic emphasis on responsibility, and on the new institutionalism, with its belief in the utility of networks. It includes a vision of a welfare state that, first, requires individuals to fulfil their duties in return for receiving their rights and, second, delivers these rights through networks based on relations of trust. It implies that the state should tackle social exclusion and network poverty by promoting individual responsibility in relation to work and family, and by taking on an enabling role in partnerships with private and voluntary sector organizations. The state should act, in this view, to ensure a stable macro-economic environment and to revitalise the supply-side of the economy through the promotion of training and networks.

Assessment and critique

Commentators have offered a number of assessments of New Labour. Typically they tell us about the effectiveness of New Labour's policies or how well the policies conform to specified values. Although I have considerable sympathy for many of them, I am struck by how often they are expressed in terms that appear to replicate the appeal to expertise by which liberal socialists legitimate restricted accounts of democracy as the election of representatives. Assessments of the New Labour often proceed by means of atomisation, comparison, and classification, all of which serve to objectify aspects of human life so as to lend an aura of expertise to the conclusions thus reached. I have already suggested how this mode of assessment dominates the debate as to whether or not New Labour is properly socialist: the whole debate is, after all, about how to classify New Labour in relation to a reified concept of socialism. Perhaps the clearest examples of this mode of assessment are, however, those collections of essays in which each author considers New Labour's record in a given policy area in which he or she claims to have expertise. The Department of Government at Manchester University has produced one such collection. 'It was agreed,' the editors write, 'that individual members of staff would examine the policy areas of most interest to them guided by two simple questions: what did New Labour promise, and what have they delivered so far?'[3] The crucial point about the Manchester collection is the division of the essays by policy area and the mode of evaluation that this implies is on offer. The collection clearly does not consist of a series of narratives of New Labour written from avowedly different perspectives. On the contrary, while there are one or two exceptions, the essays typically present themselves as theoretically innocent accounts of empirical facts. New Labour is atomised into discreet promises made in distinct policy areas; experts then assess its effectiveness in delivering on the promises. The collection is meant to be, its cover tells us, 'systematic', 'comprehensive', 'an audit'; it is not supposed to be perspectival, argumentative, or—at least in the sense I will soon describe—critical.

Atomisation, objectification, and claims to expertise are ubiquitous features of assessments of New Labour. It is worth pausing to ask why this might be a matter of concern. Surely we should not condemn the very idea of assessment? The moral is not that we should avoid generalisations and abstractions, but that we should strive to ensure that those we adopt are historicist rather than essentialist. Instead of quibbling over the historicist purity of assessments of New Labour, we might ask about their limitations as a mode of critique. The reliance on atomisation, classification, and objectification often encourages, as in the Manchester collection, a concern to provide an audit of the strengths and weaknesses of government policies. Although audits can be a perfectly acceptable mode of assessment—notably if they are aware of their own historicity—they still limit critique to faultfinding. The critic identifies one or more faults, whether big or small, in the policies of the government: perhaps New Labour does not contain the concept of equality the critic favours; or perhaps it does not prompt policies to tackle what the critic thinks are the root causes of unemployment. Faultfinding is a passing of judgement on the merits of a thing from a perspective that gestures at a given ethical or instrumental ideal from which the thing departs.

The limitations of faultfinding as a mode of critique become clear if we ask what follows from taking historicism seriously. To begin, we might examine the implications of the particularity of our own positions as critics of New Labour. Once we allow our criticisms are infused with our theoretical assumptions, we might become hesitant to find fault; we might be wary of treating our particular theoretical perspective as a valid one from which to judge others. This hesitation might give rise to self-reflexive moments in our assessments of New Labour, moments that suggest our criticisms arise against the background of theoretical commitments that others might not share. Perhaps we might recognise that we are offering a narrative that is itself just one among a field of possible narratives. We thereby would move from faultfinding to critique. Instead of evaluating New Labour in terms of apparently given concepts, values, or facts, we would juxtapose rival narratives or ask what should follow from a set of concepts we happen to share with particular others.

Next we might examine the implications of the particularity of New Labour as the object of our critique. All too often political ideas or movements present themselves as based on neutral truths whether these be facts or values. Critique, as I am using the term, consists less of an evaluation of its object, than in the act of unmasking its object as contingent or partial. It might unmask the contingency of its object by showing it to be one among a field of possible narratives. Or it might unmask the partiality of its object by showing how it arises against the background of an inherited tradition that is held by, or even benefits, a particular group within society. Critique often has a clear evaluative import in that by unmasking the contingency and the partiality of its object, it portrays its object as being mistaken about its own nature or as eliding its own nature in the interests of a group or class. Because critique thus privileges unmasking over evaluation, it tends to rely on philosophical or historical analysis. Critique deploys philosophical analysis to unpack the conceptual presuppositions of a movement or practice. It deploys historical analysis to unpack the roots of these presuppositions in particular traditions, debates, or other such contexts. We move from fault-finding to critique when we shift our attention from the evaluation of a movement or practice in terms of a given set of criteria to the use of philosophical and historical analyses to bring into view the very theories or concepts that inform its nature and its own evaluations.

The preceding account of New Labour is intended, then, to act as a critique as well as an explanation. We can explain the broad contours of New Labour's ideas and policies as a liberal socialist response to issues highlighted by the New Right but conceived in ways indebted to the new institutionalism and communitarianism. This narrative of New Labour renders it a contingent triumph of a particular web of beliefs, not a product of a 'rational' politics of catch-up or a 'path dependent' development of socialism for new times. It also contrasts with New Labour's portrayal of itself as having broken with old ideological dogmatisms of state and market so as to adopt a pragmatic stance focused on the effectiveness of policy instruments in delivering ends. It suggests, on the contrary, that New Labour's professed pragmatism disguises a theoretical bias, taken from new institutionalism, in favour of networks as an alternative to hierarchies and markets.

Democratic alternatives?

New Labour emerged as a response to dilemmas such as inflation and welfare dependency against the background of liberal socialism. Hence liberal socialist themes remain prominent in its practices. New Labour is wedded, for example, to concepts of community and state that are ultimately monolithic, unitary ones. It seems unsympathetic to the pluralism associated with non-governmental traditions of socialism. Even when it appeals to networks to deliver services, it tends to focus on the techniques by which the central state might try to impose itself in order to define both patterns of behaviour and eventual outcomes. New Labour remains wedded to policy-making processes that privilege experts in the context of representative democracy. It has turned to networks, for example, because experts—the new institutionalists and policy-wonks influenced by them—maintain that networks are an effective form of service delivery. Indeed, it invokes participation as a means to efficiency and effectiveness at least as much as a way to extend democracy.

The important point here is that critique foregrounds other strands of socialism that provide resources with which to develop alternatives. New Labour, following the dominant tradition in the party, remains wedded to a liberal account of democracy as representative government; it makes comparatively little reference to other forms of popular control over the executive or associations in civil society. Yet, other strands of British socialism include a different analysis of freedom as inherently embedded in particular practices. Non-governmental socialists have concentrated attention on the ways people make their freedom through deliberation and participation in a range of practices. What, we might ask, would be a deliberative and participatory alternative to New Labour? Few non-governmental socialists want to repudiate liberal rights and liberties; they want only to supplement them. In their view, freedom is not only abstract rights and liberties under the rule of law; it is also a concrete practice. So, while they might endorse many aspects of liberal democracy, they typically do so as part of an account of a practice of freedom that in other respects departs from liberal democracy. A suitable practice of freedom requires, they might argue, that we can debate and remake even these liberal rights and mechanisms; it requires that we adopt other rights and devices so as to extend democracy to other areas of social life; and it requires that we decentre the state, perhaps handing aspects of governance over to other associations.

Mark Bevir

Notes

1. This essay offers a brief statement of themes developed more fully in Mark Bevir, *New Labour: A Critique* (London, 2005).
2. Logie Barrow and Ian Bullock, *Democratic Ideas and the British Labour Movement, 1880–1914* (Cambridge, 1966).
3. David Coates and Peter Lawler, 'Preface', to Coates and Lawler (eds), *New Labour in Power* (Manchester, 2000), p.ix.

Margaret Thatcher's Conservative Party—midwife of the New Labour project

One of Margaret Thatcher's lasting and unacknowledged achievements was her substantial contribution to the creation of the New Labour project under Tony Blair. Indeed, she can claim with some justification to be its successful midwife. During her years as prime minister between May 1979 and November 1990 Mrs Thatcher transformed British politics. The profound economic and social reforms that she pushed through brought an end to the so-called post-war settlement that had dominated the political system since 1945, although with increasing difficulty. Her success proved to be total. The Labour Party—with the loss of four consecutive general elections—was compelled to respond, not only by accepting most of her legacy and that of her successor John Major but also by embracing its ideological core with growing enthusiasm.

Under Blair's leadership after July 1994 the Labour Party guaranteed the new Thatcherite or neo-liberal consensus that was established in the 1980s. The anti-trade union industrial relations legislation and the privatisation of most of the country's nationalised industries was accepted by Blair and his colleagues. There was going to be no attempt at any return to the managed corporate capitalism of the post-war years. They also agreed to maintain a forty per cent upper basic rate on earnings for payment of income tax and the deregulation and liberalisation of financial and other services. Market forces were to determine the well-being of the political economy. A commitment to the provision of private finance initiatives to help in improvements in investment projects and other programmes for the modernisation of hospitals and schools was also stressed by the incoming Labour government.

For the first time in nearly eighty years the country's mainstream political parties now accepted and agreed to work within the ideological assumptions of free market capitalism. Blair and his chancellor Gordon Brown, despite their personal differences, were united by their mutual conviction that Britain must be turned into a competitive and dynamic country that could respond effectively to the growing demands of increasing globalisation with open markets and the creation of a more dynamic enterprise culture . This is the remarkable consequence of the Thatcher years. Labour's landslide general election victory in May 1997 did not really represent a radical shift in political direction for the country comparable to what had happened in 1906, 1945 or 1979. On the contrary, Tony Blair swept into 10 Downing Street on a cautious and modest programme of continuity and consolidation, even to the extent of swallowing the outgoing Conservative government's public expenditure plans for his first three years in office. In government, New Labour actually extended the Thatcher agenda over a wide swathe of policy—from the transfer to the private sector of remaining publicly owned enterprises such as air traffic control and the London underground, to a managerial shake-up of the public service sector founded on performance targets and benchmarking.

It is true that sporadic attempts have been made since May 1997 to explain that New Labour is nothing more than a distinctive and modernising form of European Social Democracy. The so-called Third Way was hailed as a sensible synthesis of social equity and economic efficiency which somehow avoided both the harshness of Thatcher's doctrinaire approach to politics and the dogmas of a democratic socialism that was roundly denounced by the new triumphalist Blair government as Old Labour. But in truth, Blair's primary personal contribution to the evolution of British politics was to accept the Thatcher inheritance in all its basic essentials. Ironically in doing so he has led the Labour Party back into the mainstream and transformed it into the natural party of government, an ambition that eluded his predecessors—Clem Attlee and Harold Wilson. At the same time, the Conservative Party has been forced onto the margins of British politics.

The origins of this astonishing reversal in the fortunes of the country's mainstream parties do not lie so much in the internal politics of the Labour Party after John Smith's death in March 1994 but in the discussions and actions of the Conservatives during their period in opposition between March 1974 and May 1979 and thereafter through their lengthy uninterrupted years in government.

Margaret Thatcher was always determined to put an end to the consensus politics of the post-war years and she never really denied that this was her ultimate objective. It is true that her radical instincts for fundamental change were always constrained in practice by the need to work amicably with many senior cabinet colleagues who did not necessarily share her attitude. Her room for manoeuvre was also limited by the harshness of the economic times as registered unemployment climbed to over three million in the early 1980s. But she never left anybody in serious doubt that what she wanted to do was to turn Britain once more into a thriving and successful capitalist country, freed from what she saw as a crippling bureaucratic and appeasing culture of industrial politics that she believed had pandered to obstructive trade union power and undermined the free market system.

Fundamental transformation

Her ambitions were undoubtedly transformational. But she was not satisfied to bring about changes that would only last as long as the life of a Conservative government. She wanted to ensure that the results would prove to be long-lasting and irreversible and therefore not suffer from any inevitable reversal with the return of the Labour Party to government in the future. What was required to ensure this would happen was to bring about a fundamental transformation in the Labour Party so that it also embraced free markets, private enterprise, profits and competition and encouraged a rugged individualism that required low levels of personal taxation and embraced wealth and rewards for the successful and the risk takers. There was to be no master plan. But the boldness of the Thatcher vision cannot be doubted. Her intention was not only to rid Britain of what she regarded as its defeatist and debilitating post-war social settlement but to ensure the Labour Party came to accept and embrace her achievements. Insufficient attention has so far been given by contemporary historians to the strategies of the Conservatives in the late 1970s and in government in breaking the mould of British politics. By making Labour safe for capitalism Mrs Thatcher was able to achieve her overriding purpose.

It is not possible to point directly to a key speech or document in which she unveiled her intentions so openly, even if she made much of it implicit. But her close friend and colleague Sir Keith Joseph had no doubt of what her Conservative Party needed to do in the long term. Indeed, he should take the real credit for what happened.

On 10 July 1975 Joseph, who was then Conservative shadow trade and industry spokesman, made a fascinating contribution to the internal debate of the party on what its future ideological direction should be. It is worth quoting extensively. Joseph laid down a set of 'guiding themes' that he argued his party should champion in its programmes and manifestoes. These were as follows:

> Strengthening choice and responsibility for the individual and the family. Standing up for the unorganised non-union majority of the workforce who have been hit on the head by inflation. Defending free enterprise and the system of economic freedom against further doctrinal attack from the left while at the same time humanising market forces to make a compassionate society both equality of respect and equality of opportunity. Spreading the ownership of wealth and prosperity in such a way as to facilitate personal saving and the transfer of modest amounts of personal wealth. Concentrating social provision on those in genuine need thus asserting our credentials as a compassionate party with a record of effective care.

Joseph also believed the party must stand up for the rule of law with 'the right of individuals and groups to exercise their freedom within the law'. He was also convinced the Conservatives should take a much tougher attitude to immigration and crime.

The list of Joseph's 'themes' strike an uncanny recognition for those who read the publications of the Blair Labour Party. Indeed, in some ways his 'guiding themes' look more progressive. In the late 1970s Joseph's analysis was wrongly derided by the Labour government of the time as extremist and lacking in credibility. In fact, much of its populism resonated with key sections of the British manual working class employed in the private sector, who were facing a wage squeeze due to government incomes policy and a tax burden on their incomes. Joseph and Thatcher were no ideologues out of touch with the rest of British society. Indeed, under their direction the party was about to become the political beneficiary of a fundamental shift in the loyalties and attitudes of millions of working-class voters. It is often overlooked that the Conservatives under Thatcher made a significant and unprecedented advance into the manual working-class vote in the May 1979 general election. This did not happen fortuitously. On the contrary, the outcome owed much to the impact on party policy of intensive polling and interviewing carried out for the Conservatives by independent market researchers, mainly under the direction of the Conservative Research Department. While the Labour Party at this time dismissed such forecasting as irrelevant or damaging to its ideological messages as it moved leftwards, the Conservatives were able to construct a credible and effective picture of what was happening to British society during the 1970s. To Thatcher's undoubted relief, they found that key parts of the manual working class were sympathetic to her fundamental ideological messages. Denis Healey once famously described Mrs Thatcher as the *Pasionaria* of the English middle classes. But her electoral appeal stretched far beyond the leafy suburbs of southern England.

The party's private polling that was carried out in the late 1970s found widespread discontent among Labour voters, especially young, male and skilled manual workers. This key group rejected government imposed national incomes policies that restrained their wage increases and narrowed their pay relativities and differentials and prevented genuine collective bargaining between their trade unions and employers. So did Mrs Thatcher. They disliked the high marginal rate of income tax that squeezed their earnings. The Conservative's promised tax cutting agenda was highly attractive to them. Although many may have been trade union members, they were opposed to the partisan politics of their elected leaders who claimed to represent them. There was a particular resentment among workers employed in the private sector at the aggressively disruptive antics of public sector unions like the National Union of Public Employees, especially during the 1978–9 'winter of discontent'. Opinion polls found overwhelming support among working-class voters for curbs on mass picketing, the abolition of the closed shop and the need for more democratic procedures in trade unions through the use of the secret ballot in union elections and before the calling of official strikes. Mrs Thatcher promised action on all those areas, albeit cautiously before 1981 and the arrival of Norman Tebbit at the Department of Employment. The Conservative promise to enable council-house tenants to buy their own homes at discount prices was hugely popular across the working classes. A tough stance on law and order and a more resolute attitude to immigration also found a sympathetic following among traditional Labour voters. As Professor Anthony King was to observe, never had an opposition party so penetrated the values and beliefs of the core supporters of their main rival.

Menacing waters

Again, Sir Keith Joseph was the most perceptive of the Conservative leadership in his appreciation of what such findings meant for the future success of his party. Labour was turning away from any positive response to the new economic and social realities. Its growing belief in what came to be known as the Alternative Economic Strategy failed to impress many working-class voters. Joseph was convinced that the Labour Party had become incapable of effective government as it demanded ever growing state control and ownership over the political economy. He believed that the dominance of the trade unions over Labour policy-making was more than just a temporary shift in the balance of internal power in the party. However, the trade unions were deeply hostile to enterprise and profit-making. They did not believe in a market economy. Their concept of socialism was almost as damaging to the country as that of the rising Labour left under Tony Benn. In the past, the Conservatives had often sought to demonise the Labour Party's commitment to socialism but this was essentially rhetorical in its intent. It was hard to suggest Labour was a threat to the British way of life when it was dominated by stern patriots like Attlee, Ernest Bevin, Herbert Morrison, Hugh Gaitskell and Harold Wilson. Now in the late 1970s, Joseph believed the Labour Party was moving into menacing waters and it was therefore increasingly vulnerable to Conservative accusations of unreason and dogma.

In his privately made arguments in the late 1970s and early 1980s, Joseph asserted that Labour's difficulties were partly structural. The party would have to either break its historic links to the trade unions or at the very least reduce the power of collective producer interests in its policy-making procedures. It would also have to abandon its commitment—under clause four section four of its 1918 constitution—to a planned collectivist economy based on state-owned enterprises. The existence of that clause made it impossible for the Labour Party to become truly social-democratic and thereby a willing participant in the advance of a free-market economy, Joseph reasoned. His clinical analysis of the peculiar and distinctive nature of the Labour movement was combined with a conviction that the Conservatives needed to bring about what would amount to the creation of a new Labour Party that repudiated socialism and its trade union connections. Joseph and Thatcher were realistic enough to recognise that their party could not expect to enjoy perpetual one-party rule. While in 1979 they were convinced their planned transformation of Britain would require a prolonged period in government for the Conservatives, they acknowledged Labour would eventually return to office. But they were keen to ensure that the centre-left party by that time would no longer be committed to any form of democratic socialism.

Joseph envisaged the emergence of a Labour Party that believed in free enterprise, was patriotic in defence, firm on law and order, keen to reward enterpreurial success, opposed to state controls in industry and finance, in favour of low levels of personal taxation. It was to be moderate and responsible, dominated by the national and not by class interests. Like the Democrats in the USA, the Labour Party would accept the basic aims of market capitalism. Under Neil Kinnock and then John Smith Labour moved slowly and cautiously in that direction as its basic policies failed to win popular approval with the electorate. Under Blair the pace quickened. By May 1997 the party looked very much like the model progressive party that had been envisaged by Joseph nearly twenty years earlier. Indeed, in its great victory at that time Labour recaptured much of the working-class vote in southern England that it had lost in the late 1970s while at the same time it was appealing to the middle classes far beyond those employed in the public sector. Thanks to Mrs Thatcher, the party was once again a national political force capable of dominating the country.

Robert Taylor

Reviews

Jean-François Fayet, *Karl Radek (1885–1939): Biographie politique* (Peter Lang, Bern, 2004), ISBN 3–906770–31–1, 813pp., £55.

We already had a good biography of Radek—Warren Lerner's *Karl Radek, the Last Internationalist*, published by Stanford University Press in 1970. But that was a slim volume of 240 pages, whereas this book, by a Swiss historian, is more than three times as long. Fayet was able to use the Soviet archives now open to researchers and also those of the former GDR. He has also drawn on much Radek-related literature published since 1970, such as Pierre Broué's *Révolution en Allemagne 1917–1923* and Curt Geyer's *Die Revolutionäre Illusion*. His bibliography fills forty pages.

However, the greater volume of its sources is not the only reason for the length of Fayet's book. The first quarter is devoted to the period before the Bolshevik revolution and contains much information about the German and Polish social democrats in the early years of the last century. When I noticed this, my initial reaction (shame on me!) was 'padding'; but, as I read, I realised that Fayet has given us a more complete picture than we had before of the Polish and German milieux in which Radek's political personality was formed, and which conditioned his later conduct. In the German movement he encountered philistinism and bureaucracy and in the Polish movement he suffered from intrigue and skulduggery. He reacted strongly against the former and learnt all too well from the latter, before being expelled by both. But he also discovered both the deep loyalty of the German workers to their established organisations and the force of Polish patriotism—which helps to explain his pioneering of the united-front policy and his (unheeded) warning against the Soviet invasion of ethnic Poland. All the other phases of Radek's career are similarly provided by Fayet with plenty of background.

The Radek who emerges from these pages does not substantially differ from the figure already familiar to us, although we may now understand him

better. He is still the complete 'rootless cosmopolitan', the modern embod-
iment of the legendary 'wandering Jew', a gift for antisemitic caricaturists,
still the bohemian notorious for contrariness and scurrility. And still the man
who astonished comrades by his wit, his erudition, his command of languages (though, apparently, he never learnt more Yiddish than he had to in
order to tell dirty jokes in it) and his ability to turn out, quickly and to order,
well-researched and highly readable articles on a wide range of subjects.

Fayet, like Lerner, emphasises Radek's *essential* internationalism, intensi-
fied as it was by his lack of a firm basis in the labour movement of any
particular country. This marked him to the end, so that, even in his dis-
graceful 1934 hagiography of Stalin ('The Architect of Socialist Society') he
could not refrain from claiming that, by establishing 'socialism in one country taken separately', the Soviet dictator was building 'a fortress facilitating
the international victory of socialism'. In the final words of his text, Fayet
writes of 'Germany, which had never ceased to be the political passion of
[Radek's] life'. The sections of the book dealing with Radek in relation to
German affairs are, for this reviewer, the most valuable.

The support given by the German masses to the government's war in 1914
helped Radek to shake off his Luxemburgist illusions and become a Leninist,
and his experiences in Leningrad tempered him further politically. When he
returned to Germany as a Bolshevik he strove to prevent a repetition in Berlin,
by the local hotheads, of the July 1917 near-disaster in Russia's capital. He
was appalled by the Spartakist revolt in January 1919. Fayet is not convinced
by Fel'shtinsky's allegation (in 1997) that Radek may have been spared exe-
cution by his military captors after that event in return for giving away the
hiding places of Liebknecht and Luxemburg. He thinks that those who would
indeed have liked to kill him (*'Karl, Rosa, Radek, sind ihr nicht dabei?'*) restrained
themselves because of his position in the Soviet government, whose interest they intended to cultivate. Here, perhaps, was the beginning of that role
which Radek was to play in the early 1920s in the negotiations between Soviet
Russia and the Reichswehr for mutual aid in an alliance based on their common desire to disrupt the Versailles peace settlement.

For his criticism of the Spartakist revolt Radek came under attack from
Béla Kun, who accused him of 'revolutionary pessimism', and this led him
to cover himself on the left by writing, in 1920, articles in defence of the
ill-fated Soviet republics in Bavaria and Hungary, articles in which he took
the line that communists have to be with the workers wherever they are fighting, even in a foredoomed battle. As Fayet points out, this was in total
contradiction with his attitude in Berlin's 'Bloody Week'. Radek was opposing the line of the outstanding German communist Paul Levi, who had

dismissed the events in Munich and Budapest as mere putsches. It was the first sign of a split between two men whose political outlooks had much in common, though their personalities could hardly have been more different.

To Radek's misfortune, the Executive Committee of the Communist International was presided over at this time by Zinoviev—not only a personal enemy but also a promoter of left policies which Radek felt to be fallacious. Having, as Fayet points out, 'no legitimacy but what the Comintern gave him', Radek was obliged to keep in with the Zinovievists when they were acting against the spirit of policies that he supported—the workers' united front and communist support for 'workers' governments'. He was obliged, therefore, again to distance himself from Levi, on the question of the purge of 'rights' from the Italian communist party. By easing the path for sectarianism, this helped create the situation that Mussolini exploited successfully in 1922. On the 'March Action' in Germany he was careful, also, to take an ambiguous position which saved him from sharing Levi's fate of expulsion.

Fayet follows Richard Lowenthal in emphasising the importance of the phase beginning in 1921 in the history of the Comintern, which he sees as the real start of 'bolshevisation', usually dated from 1924. Radek helped, in this period, to foster a habit of automatic subordination of the national parties to Moscow's rulings, and the consequent regime under which he was himself eventually crushed.

Radek's best-remembered speech is certainly his eulogy of the 'fascist' martyr Schlageter, in 1923. There was a dual background to this. On the one hand, Radek's dealings, on behalf of the Soviet government, with the German military had shown the possibility of communist co-operation with the nationalist elements which, perhaps, he overestimated. On the other hand, as a sophisticated student of politics, he was one of the few in Comintern circles who appreciated the *novelty* of fascism, the fact that it was not just another variant of bourgeois reaction (as Zinoviev affirmed, along with calling social democracy a wing of fascism), and that combating it called for fresh thinking and bold initiatives.

The 'Schlageter line' may not have been the right one to win over the fascist rank and file (perhaps there was no way?) but it did constitute an attempt to solve the problem, which others merely neglected. However, struggle to attract the fascist masses by sharing their 'national' concerns conflicted with struggle for a united front with the social democrats, who favoured a policy of 'fulfilment' of Germany's obligations, and it alarmed the French and Czechoslovakian communists. But it was only a sharper expression of an attitude implicit, and sometimes explicit, in Soviet foreign policy since 1919.

Fayet is wrong to claim (p.453, *n.*551) that Radek was the first communist to speak of Germany as 'a colony of the Entente'. Lenin had said that the Treaty of Versailles had reduced Germany to a state of 'colonial dependence', and had instructed the delegates to the Genoa Conference in 1922 to study Keynes's notorious gift to German *revanchiste* propaganda, *The Economic Consequences of the Peace*.

Radek knew better than to go with the dream of a proletarian revolution in the Germany of 1923 and at first made his view clear. But then, as in 1921, he fell abjectly into line with the Comintern and Soviet leadership, who demanded something spectacular to compensate for the failure of Bulgarian communists to defend Stambulisky against Tsankov in June. In this connection, Fayet is able to draw on the minutes of the decisive politburo meeting of 20–22 August.

The book's last sections cover Radek's 'China' period and his involvement with the Left Opposition, then his return to (qualified) favour with Stalin after he had capitulated, when the only 'awakening of the masses' he could foresee as likely was a revolt of the peasantry that would threaten the 'gains of October'. To Radek was now given the task of signalling to the world that the USSR was about to make a major turn in foreign policy.

Pravda carried, on 10 May 1933, an article from his pen which claimed that 'revisions of the Treaty of Versailles means war'. This reviewer remembers reading the English translation of it which appeared in R. P. Dutt's *Labour Monthly* for June 1933. (Some eyebrows were raised, but most of us failed, I think, to appreciate fully what was being heralded—a possible alignment with the hated 'Entente' states against the Soviets' old ally.) Fayet notes (p.680) that, in accordance with Stalin's two-track policy in the period now opened, Radek told the German ambassador in January 1934 not to suppose that 'everything has been decided…We shall do nothing that would make it permanently impossible for us to return to a common policy with Germany'.

Radek appears to have died in a brawl in a Siberian prison camp in 1939, though whether this was before or after the signing of the Stalin-Hitler pact is not clear.

Brian Pearce

Charles Ashleigh, *The Rambling Kid. A Novel About the IWW* with an introduction by Steve Kellerman (Charles H. Kerr, Chicago, 2003), ISBN 0–88286–272–3, 302pp., $17 pbk.

Charles Ashleigh's only novel was published originally in Britain in 1930. Whilst not a great work of fiction it is a significant historical document. In this edition Ashleigh's life is also outlined by Steve Kellerman in an excellent and informative introduction to the novel.

An appreciation of its value can begin with the experiences of the author. Ashleigh was born in London in 1888. Despite his parents separating when he was six, his childhood was economically secure and he had a solid education at Brighton Grammar School, and at schools in Lausanne and Hanover. A commitment to socialism came early. From his mid-teens, he sampled a variety of socialist organisations—the Independent Labour Party, the Social Democratic Federation, the Fabian Society and the Clarion Scouts. He linked to the circle around the radical weekly, the *New Age*. A street propagandist immersed in an Edwardian socialist kaleidoscope, he had no enduring attachment to any specific organisation.

From 1909, he was a member of the English-speaking socialist diaspora, that linked together socialist initiatives in the British Isles, the Americas, southern Africa, and Australia. One medium was the publications of Charles H. Kerr of Chicago. Ashleigh took a post as a railway clerk in Argentina and helped to form socialist groups within Buenos Aires' English-speaking community. He travelled to the United States in 1912, jumping ship in Portland, Oregon and became a paid speaker for the Socialist Party of America. This was the year when the SPA's presidential candidate, Eugene Debs, secured over 900,000 votes, six per cent of the total poll. This limited advance offered some encouragement to American socialists after years of painstaking propaganda. Yet Ashleigh quickly left the party and joined the Industrial Workers of the World, the 'Wobblies'.

The IWW were syndicalists; they ignored, or at best marginalised, political activities in favour of militant industrial campaigns informed by the precept that the workers' real power lay at the point of production. The organisation was firmly socialist and aggressively democratic. Scornful of the respectable American Federation of Labor, it recruited amongst those whom AFL affiliated unions neglected or despised—newly arrived immigrants, itinerant workers, and to a degree, Afro-Americans. Ashleigh became an 'organiser-at-large', actively proclaiming the message of the IWW amongst diverse groups of workers.

A combination of limited income and the need to travel extensively meant that he shared the experiences of fellow 'Wobblies'—riding across the continent on freight trains, harassment and beatings at the hands of railway police and vigilantes, the risk of gaol. This was a masculine world of bonding against shared adversaries. Ashleigh was empowered and shaped by an optimism and solidarity that characterised IWW culture in its heroic moment. Yet the threat from enemies could go beyond beatings and gaol. Ashleigh organised the publicity for the IWW defenders, following the Everett, Washington massacre in November 1916. Certainly five, and possibly twelve, 'Wobblies' were killed by vigilantes; but it was IWW members who were tried for murder, a grotesque episode that ended in their acquittal.

The Everett bloodletting was a barbaric response by business interests to IWW attempts to organise north western timber trade workers. After the United States entered the European war in April 1917, repression became much more thorough. IWW members hoped to exploit the opportunities presented in strategic industries to improve wages and conditions. Employers could utilise patriotic hysteria to enlist the aid of the Federal Government, a strategy facilitated by the anti-war rhetoric, if not practice, of many 'Wobbly' speakers and journalists. In September 1917, 184 'Wobblies' were arrested; they included Ashleigh. Beginning appropriately on All Fools Day 1918, he and 112 of his comrades stood trial in Chicago on lengthy indictments. Naively, many defendants seemed to believe that a combination of the rule of law and lack of evidence would offer ample protection. The jury listened to the proceedings until mid-August; they then took less than one hour to reach uniformly guilty verdicts on ten thousand separate charges.

Show trial verdicts were succeeded by draconian sentences. Ashleigh was sentenced to ten years in prison with a $30,000 fine. He served time with hard labour in Leavenworth Penitentiary, Kansas. The authorities' vengeance against radicals did not die with the end of the war in Europe. The Palmer Raids early in 1920 demonstrated a desire to destroy the remains of the American left. But at the end of 1921, Ashleigh along with other foreign nationals accepted a deal-release and deportation.

His farewell to the United States was his farewell to the 'Wobblies'. Exponents of syndicalism had divided in their responses to the Bolshevik Revolution, and the establishment of the Communist International. In particular the survival of the Soviet state gave credibility to the emerging wisdom that a disciplined revolutionary party offered the only route to a socialist society. This doctrine, increasingly codified in an emerging canon of approved texts, seemed an authoritative challenge to the syndicalist outlook. Ashleigh, returning to Europe, joined the British Communist Party and embraced the new wisdom. His linguistic and journalistic abilities made him a valuable recruit. In the mid-1920s he worked in Berlin as press chief for the Red International of Labour Unions (Profintern); in the early 1930s he edited an English language paper in Moscow, the *Moscow Daily News*. Yet alongside his formal communist orthodoxy, he retained something of the convention-challenging iconoclasm that had characterised the IWW. In particular, Ashleigh's open homosexuality grated against the authoritarianism and official puritanism of Stalin's Russia. He was sacked as editor of the *Moscow Daily News* and expelled from the Soviet Union in 1934. He, together with other British and German comrades, were supposedly guilty of corrupting Soviet youth. He retained his party card until his death in 1974, but his influence had effectively ended.

Ashleigh's American experiences provided raw material for *The Rambling Kid*, but the novel is not autobiographical. Unlike Ashleigh, the novel's protagonist, Joe Crane, is unambiguously working class. He grows up in a tenement in London's East End before the 1914–18 war. His father, Frank, is a docker subject to the unpredictabilities and humiliations of casualisation. Frank Crane, 'a transplanted peasant who has never grown used to the industrial life' (p.8), dreams of returning to the countryside, a lost Eden from which he had been expelled by the priorities of a new landlord. The Crane family escape from the East End through an individualistic device characteristic of nineteenth-century fiction, an unexpected legacy.

Seduced by misleading letters from cousins who have crossed the Atlantic, they travel steerage class, eventually to farm in South Dakota. But they experience further demoralisation. Frank Crane proves an inadequate farmer, but more significantly the farm is heavily mortgaged and repayments cannot be met. The bank forecloses; Joe moves with his mother and younger siblings to Minneapolis; his father stays in the countryside as a labourer. The American dream has shattered as has the belief that 'back to the land' offers salvation. The Cranes must survive as members of the American working class. Joe's parents do so pragmatically. Rose Crane is employed part-time as a domestic servant. Frank eventually returns to the city as a flour mill worker. In contrast Joe despairs of steady employment in Minneapolis. In part this reflects rising expectations; he had learned shorthand from a friendly neighbouring farmer. Physically tough from his Dakota farm work and attracted by the conviviality of itinerant workers in Minneapolis, he decides to join them.

At this point in the novel Joe Crane has been brought to a position in some respects equivalent to that of Charles Ashleigh when he joined the IWW at the end of 1912. Joe too becomes a 'Wobbly'; but in contrast to Ashleigh, Joe was not a politically conscious figure. He had experienced urban and rural poverty and the disillusions of the failed farming venture; but as yet this is simply understood as individual and family misfortune. The passages that follow are the most evocative in the book: the camaraderie of IWW camps, tales and songs; the fear of missing a footing when illegally boarding a train; encounters with authority ending in victory and laughter or in defeat. Joe and his comrades travel the rails westwards to bring in the harvest. As Ashleigh insisted they played a vital economic role—'through bitter cold and smoke and turmoil, danger of arrest or of a beating—towards the harvest jobs that would earn them sustenance for a short space, and help provide the world with bread' (p.99). IWW organisation could mean the bidding up of wages with farmers desperate to bring in the harvest; such coups could earn the enmity of local business.

Even within this celebration of 'Wobbly' solidarity, there intrudes the hindsight resulting from Ashleigh's shift to Third International communism. The IWW is criticised from the standpoint of communist orthodoxy in 1930, the high noon of Comintern 'Class against Class' strategy. Lenin's *What Is To Be Done?* had recently been translated into English and the true communist recognised the necessity for the revolutionary party pursuing the correct strategy. Ashleigh characterises Joe as not a 'good organisation man'. He kept to IWW roles and read their newspaper but—'he failed altogether…to realise the fundamental social criticism, and the revolutionary implications of the IWW (p.110). But Ashleigh acknowledges that Joe was not solely responsible for this inadequacy: 'The literature and the exponents of the organisation were often contradictory and vague. They failed to bridge the gap between the obviously needful tasks of organising the workers, so as to get higher wages, lower hours and better conditions, and the too sketchy utopianism of the final revolutionary objective' (ibid.). The criticism is reinforced by a presentation of the divers IWW responses to American entry into the European war, both in terms of the substantive question, and the feasibility of any oppositional response.

After the harvest Joe with his mates 'Blackie' and 'Elsie' sets out for California, once again riding the rails. 'Elsie', from a progressive bourgeois family in Minneapolis, is shot by a cop. Joe's visceral hostility to 'the goddamn dirty bastards' grows (p.169). But hatred is not enough. He begins to seek rigorous understanding wrestling with texts in economics and history, a counterweight to the delights of San Francisco. 'He had been reading a lot; props had fallen in the galleries of his mind; great masses of rubble had descended and had been carried away. New thoughts, washing away old landmarks. New lights, revealing unknown reaches' (p.179). This budding autodidact meets a Russian revolutionary Nalid, an IWW member who has rejected the Wobblies' antipathy to politics, and has retained his membership of the Socialist Party. Nalid argues for a militant working-class response to American entry into the war, but expresses scepticism about its likelihood. Reference points are beginning to shift in the novel. The American working class may be incapable of an effective anti-war politics; workers may need to look elsewhere. 'The IWW hasn't any basic theory. We all differ with regard to war; we differ regarding the Russian Revolution of Kerensky, and the Russian Revolution of the Bolsheviks which is soon going to happen if I am any judge' (pp.183–4). For Nalid the challenge of revolutionary politics necessitates 'officers…realists not dreamers' (pp.184–5)—the antithesis of the IWW. He dismisses the 'Wobblies' as 'a ragged crowd of guerrilla fighters—going up against highly organised capitalism with its powerful government' (p.184).

The screw tightens. The novel's setting is now the immediate prelude to the mass arrests of the 'Wobblies' in September 1917. Joe avoids becoming a defendant in a show trial by a combination of chance and conspiracy. Previously arrested as the room mate of 'Blackie' who has embarked on a policy of robbing members of the San Francisco bourgeoisie, he is released on bail just as the net tightens on the IWW. Joe goes underground; he is becoming a special kind of revolutionary—'hearts of steel and wills of steel' (p.261). Prior to the Bolshevik Revolution he is a Bolshevik in the making. Apart from his politicisation his shorthand skills are a distinctive asset. At a meeting in Chicago he is informed that he has been selected in anticipation of a Bolshevik Revolution. He should travel to Russia to participate in the formation of a new revolutionary International; he sails from Vancouver for the revolution. As a 'Wobbly' he had travelled under the name 'London Slim'. He is now 'Ivan Vaksoff'.

Increasingly didactic and with slight sense of complex characterisation, *The Rambling Kid* rises above these limitations in the chapters presenting the IWW members, working, celebrating, travelling and suffering. Ashleigh articulates something of his own experiences and feelings as an IWW organiser. Whatever his subsequent genuflections to communist orthodoxy, something of the earlier vitality remained. Immediacy is also the quality of another fictional representation of the 'Wobblies' in the early sections of John Dos Passos's *The 42nd Parallel*. Dos Passos was then on the left but not a communist. Using experiences recalled by an old 'Wobbly', Dos Passos sends Fenian McCreary across the United States on freight trains, and to Goldfield, Nevada at the height of the 1907 conflict between mineowners and 'Wobblies'. Yet Fenian is no revolutionary with heart and will of steel. He quits his comrades in Goldfield to marry his pregnant girlfriend Maisie in San Francisco. In contrast Joe Crane, alias 'Ivan Vaksoff', abandons his relationship with a Jewish socialist in the interests of the revolution. When Fenian walks out on Maisie and their two children, he is attracted by the excitement of the Mexican Revolution. There amidst political confusion he makes himself comfortable with a stenographer called Concha—'Every poor man socialista…But when you get rich quick, you all very much capitalistic' (Dos Passos, *USA*, p.261). Fuelled by cognac he and his associates drink to 'the workers, the trade unions, the partidor laborista, the social revolution and the agaristas'. He has made an individual settlement, 'south of the border', laced with radical rhetoric. This is far from the dreams of 'Ivan Vaksoff' but perhaps offers an epitaph for the 'Wobblies' to fit alongside those emphasising state repression and the divisive impact of the Bolshevik Revolution.

Comparison with Dos Passos' contemporaneous treatment of the 'Wobblies' clarifies how far Ashleigh's presentation is characteristic of a genre prevalent in approved communist biographies and autobiographies. The hero or rarely heroine has experiences that are both testing and educational. The consequence is an understanding of the world and what is to be done. Such a text can be read as a pilgrim's progress in which false friends and illusory options are exposed and the means of salvation—the revolutionary party—is revealed. Take for example, Willie Gallacher, the socialist craftsman fresh from his Clydeside campaigns, travelling to Moscow in 1920 and meeting Lenin. Gradually his contempt for parliament and parties erodes. 'The more I talked with Lenin and the other comrades, the more I came to see what the party of the workers meant in the revolutionary struggle. It was in this, the conception of the party, that the genius of Lenin had expressed itself' (Gallacher, *Revolt on the Clyde*, pp.252–3). At a less elevated fictional level, and anticipating not reflecting on the events of autumn 1917, for Gallacher read Joe Crane and for Lenin, Nalid and his Chicago comrades. As one stresses to Joe, 'our Comrade Lenin—Lenin, a name you have only heard recently, I suppose, through the American newspapers, but a name some of us have known for years'(p.278).

The juxtaposition between 'Wobblies', or more broadly syndicalists, and Bolsheviks has been employed not just by partisans of official communism, but also by their critics. John Dos Passos utilised an anti-authoritarian characterisation of the 'Wobblies' to present this defeated option as both progressive and genuinely American. Several non-communist writers who remained on the left—unlike Dos Passos—saw the contrast as indicative of the damage inflicted by Bolshevik orthodoxy on options for a radical left. Contrary to the author's formal sentiments, Ashleigh's novel offers some support for such an indictment. The vitality of the 'Wobbly' passages subverts the formulaic pronouncements about revolutionary strategy that proved in the United States to be even more fanciful than the claims of the IWW.

Yet such subversion of orthodoxy within Ashleigh's text should be a caution against a simple dichotomy. His career as a communist suggests that ex-syndicalists did not simply abandon their syndicalism when they joined the party. Whatever the orthodoxy required, there nevertheless remained powerful elements of continuity. The shift from syndicalism to communism was a complex process that varied between individuals. Critical factors included their industrial experiences, their confrontations with the state and their assessments of and attractions towards the Bolshevik Revolution. Such complexities have been analysed with sensitivity by Edward Johanningsmeier and James Barrett in two recent studies of the American communist, William Z. Foster. In contrast, Ashleigh's novel is a propagandist product of its time; but even at the peak of 'Class against Class', the orthodox autho- rial message is undercut by the powerful unsentimental presentation of the 'Wobblies'. Moscow's Foreign Languages Publishing House had not wholly replaced Charles H. Kerr of Chicago.

David Howell
University of York

Francis Wheen, *How Mumbo-Jumbo Conquered the World: A Short History of Modern Delusions* (Fourth Estate, London, 2004), ISBN 0–00–714096–7, 329pp., £16.99 hbk.

'If you think Enlightenment is a problem, wait till you've tried obscuran- tism'. Francis Wheen's volume follows up this aphorism with admirable energy and conviction, and it is disappointing indeed not to be able to com- mend it unreservedly. Eleven-twelfths of it is brilliant and the remaining twenty-odd pages (mostly in the closing chapter) are terrible. This is not, it is worth stressing, because of the objectionable nature of the statements advanced in that section, but because the standard of argument, the evidence and logic he has applied elsewhere, go out the window, to be replaced by a diatribe compounded of unsupported assertion and prejudice. One is reminded of the proverb about the spoonful of tar spoiling the barrel of honey.

But to begin with the book's very considerable merits. Tom Paulin's com- ment on Wheen's biography of Marx, quoted on the back cover, 'He has such a passionate energy and commitment that made me cheer as I read it', is apposite here as well. Wheen is a superb journalist and the book is a delight to read. The main title however is a little misleading—it is not so much an examination of how (let alone why) mumbo-jumbo conquered the world, for it lacks any great degree of analytical depth. Mostly it is a relentless expo- sure of various obscurantisms which have in recent decades plagued Anglo-American culture, as well as observations on contemporary Islamic fundamentalism. The sub-title is a more accurate indication of what the volume is about.

The eleven chapters (plus prologue and introduction) could each stand as loosely connected separate articles on different manifestations of the theme. Wheen takes as his starting point 1979, with Margaret Thatcher's election and the Khomeini revolution in Iran, suggesting that these events can be taken as harbingers of the assault on Enlightenment values and the advance of an obscurantist counter-revolution, 'a moment when the world was jolted by a violent reaction to the complacency of the existing order'. This commences his discussion of the 'voodoo revolution', the imposition of the economic nostrums embraced by Thatcher and Reagan and the detrimental consequences they produced. From this he moves on to 'Old snake-oil, new bottles', an effective trashing of the credentials of management and 'how-to' gurus, noting the preferment they received form the Thatcher/Major governments and even more so from the Blairites.

'It's the end of the world as we know it' turns to Francis Fukuyama and Samuel Huntingdon with their fashionable theses regarding the 'end of history' and the 'clash of civilizations'. In fine style Wheen swiftly demolishes their respective pretensions and highlights their historical vacuity. 'The demolition merchants of reality' opens with an account of the persecution at Cambridge University of the structuralist Colin McCabe, then confronts postmodernist theoreticians, noting that in due course they acquired, 'a power they exercised with the same Stalinist intolerance displayed a few years earlier by the crusty conservatives of Cambridge. This time however, the victims were those who could not recite the post-modern shibboleths'. '… deconstruction, which began as a heresy soon turned into a dogma, and hardened into as theology…' He refers to Yale University where its 'three "boa-deconstructors" Jacques Derrida, Paul de Man and J. Hillis Miller reigned jointly as pontificating pontiffs'. This chapter also deals with creationists and 'alien abduction' cranks, demonstrating just how frighteningly influential both these sects are in US culture, finally tying them in with the irrationalism of postmodern theory. This effectively leads into the following chapter, 'The catastrophists', which concerns astrology, junk science and mysticism and their embrace by leading figures in politics and culture.

If astrology and other intellectual junk can be regarded as harmless if worrying fun and games, the following two chapters, 'With God on our side' and 'Us and them' are in a different category, for they concern respectively US military ideology with its social ramifications, and the propaganda creation of monstrous enemies in order to keep the mechanisms of the security state turning over. 'Candles in the wind' links counter-Enlightenment with the culture of emotional incontinence and sentimentality; its centrepiece is the Princess Di cult, particularly the manifestations that followed her death, which Wheen appropriately and accurately designates as a 'blubfest'. This undoubtedly constitutes the high point of the book, for which alone the author can be forgiven for the shortcomings discussed below.

'Right is the new left' is a discussion of Blairism, its incoherence and its contradictions, mentioning *inter alia*, how speedily Blair dropped the notion of 'stakeholder economy' as soon as he appreciated that its originator, Will Hutton, was an unreconstructed Keynesian. 'Forward to the past' describes the oppression and impoverishment perpetuated by the globalisation process and its enforcers, including the IMF and the WTO.

Refreshing as these chapters are however, not all are wholly perfect. There are certain inaccuracies and dubious interpretations. On pp.105–7 Al Gore is shown to be scarcely less of a scoundrel than George Bush, but then Wheen writes that, 'Liberal Democrats warned potential Nader supporters that unless they voted for Gore as 'the lesser of two evils' they would be responsible for letting Bush into the Oval Office, a counsel of despair and desperation. Failure by the American progressives to heed that counsel of desperation has cost at least ten thousand Iraqis their lives, not to speak of hundreds from other nationalities, including Americans; for although a President Gore could scarcely have avoided attacking Afghanistan in the aftermath of September 11, there is no reason to believe that he would have invaded Iraq.

In 'Right is the new left' Wheen notes that the think tank Demos was founded by Geoff Mulgan and Martin Jacques, and refers to 'awestruck tributes to Thatcherism in *Marxism Today*'. Surely Francis Wheen, as a conscientious journalist, cannot have omitted to consult the files of *Marxism Today* rather than accept at second hand the allegations of its enemies—for that resolute enemy of Thatcherism, where the term was actually coined, contains no such 'tributes'. It does indeed carry interviews with Conservative politicians, which is not what he claims. Moreover, while Mulgan is fairly described as a member of Blair's 'intellectual harem', Wheen fails to mention that Martin Jacques broke his links with Demos when its drift became apparent and has thereafter consistently attacked Blairism.

The closing chapter, 'Voodoo revisited', opens with a splendid dissection of the malpractices of Enron, and equally significantly, the way in which financial journalists and commentators who should have known better were induced to sing its praises. Then follow the pages in which Wheen appears to reverse everything he has said beforehand, in what can best be characterised as an intemperate attack upon the left's efforts to understand the roots of Islamic fundamentalist militancy and its relationship to US international policy. In effect, left-wing commentators who have taken that line are stigmatised as giving support to Al Qaida and the Taliban. More striking than the accusations however is the shift in the author's technique. Spurning the hitherto copious damning quotations from his targets, bound together with tight logic into a devastating critique, he adopts instead a style of scattergun unsubstantiated defamation. Much of his argument here follows the line of the American journal *Dissent*, which Wheen terms 'left wing', though only a very generous stretching of definitions could classify it in that manner; and he even reproduces uncritically the opinion of the *National Review*, which it would be a euphemism to call 'ultra-right'.

Rather than pick apart every fault however, it is more interesting to enquire why Wheen should have behaved in this fashion. Regrettably, he has allowed his wholly justified and praiseworthy detestation of obscurantist fundamentalism to blind him to the necessity of understanding why it has secured such a frightening hold upon the consciousness of so many of the 'wretched of the earth'. In consequence he has produced a magnificent but severely flawed study.

Willie Thompson

Beverly J. Silver, *Forces of Labor: Workers' Movements and Globalization since 1870* (Cambridge University Press, Cambridge, 2003), ISBN 0–521–52077–0, 256pp., £16.99 pbk.

Beverly Silver has written a very ambitious and very important book. Noting the revival of labour studies and labour movements after their common crisis in the final decades of the twentieth century, Silver asks whether the revival of labour unrest and associated challenges to neo-liberal globalisation are temporary, novel protests, or a resurgence of historically more familiar waves of unrest. Rejecting crude, deterministic assertions that globalisation is an irresistible force, and noting its contradictory effects on labour movement strategies, she sets out a rigorous theoretical framework, drawing on some of the giants of radical social criticism. From Eric Olin Wright she takes categories of labour movement power: associational power (deriving from collective strength based on unions and parties); and structural power, which she divides into marketplace power (deriving from tight labour markets, not least for skills), and workplace power (deriving from control of crucial stages in production processes). From Karl Polanyi she takes the notion of pendulum-like resistance to the spread of unregulated markets, involving the decommodification and recommodification of labour through political action. From Karl Marx's analysis of labour she takes the endemic conflict between labour and capital over control of production and distribution of profit. A historical succession of crises of profitability and of legitimacy is portrayed as reflecting and producing the global formation and reformation of labour movements.

The construction of an analytical framework thus begins with the insistence that all labour movements are linked by the world division of labour and by global politics. Inter-relatedness is seen in both direct terms, for example migrant workers taking union traditions with them, and indirect terms, for example capitalists fleeing strong labour movements but creating new ones elsewhere. Here we encounter what Silver describes as the key methodological aspect of her approach: the insistence that grasping the dynamic relationship between different national cases is crucial, not merely their comparison. Hence the comparative-historical method, for all its strengths, is insufficient. 'In sum', she writes (p.29), 'the perspective adopted in this book requires an analytical strategy that is sensitive to the relational processes between key actors (labour, capital, states) in the system as a whole, as well the systemic contraints affecting those sectors.'

But how to cope with the resulting complexity? First, Silver considers but rejects the method of 'encompassing comparison' deployed by Immanuel Wallerstein in favour of an 'incorporating comparison' (after Phillip McMichael) that permits agents as sub-units in a social system to create the system itself over time, rather than merely respond to systemic stimuli. Second, causal analysis is provided by what Silver calls a 'modified version of the narrative mode' (p.30) of chronologically-elaborated explanation. Third, only certain aspects of labour movement formation are addressed, namely the impact of capitalist development, and collective labour action. Other aspects, such as ways of life and disposition (after Katznelson and Zolberg), are not regarded as central (a view some historians will no doubt challenge). Fourthly, Silver seeks an 'empirical map' offering simplified historical and national data. This last is provided by the World Labour Group database, familiar from Silver's earlier collaborations with Giovanni Arrighi, Melvyn Dubrovsky and others, whose methodology is defended at some length here. This database draws on reports of labour unrest since 1870 published in the *The Times* of London and the *New York Times*, producing almost 92,000 reports from 148 countries. At an average of less than five reports per country per year, this might seem like oversimplificiation, but the purpose is to identify trends and high points rather than provide complete comparative statistics, and the method, it is argued, has been tested against complex national materials. Silver's underlying historical knowledge is in any case deep and wide.

In this book the data is used to construct compelling analyses of the historical and geographical development of labour unrest in the automotive and textile sectors, and new growth sectors of recent years (services and education). War, as ever, emerges as the phenomenon most easily associated with peaks and troughs of labour unrest and labour-friendly reform, and a key chapter here analyses the relationship between working-class formation, labour politics, imperialism and other forms of global capitalist politics. Readers will have to discover for themselves the richness of this material— and its careful attention to contradictory effects of capitalist strategies— which can not be summarised in a short review.

Anyone looking for a simple identification of strategic tasks for labour activists from this study will, not surprisingly, be disappointed. The study rejects pessimistic commentary that writes off labour as a spent historical force, but the conclusion is careful not to spin dramatic predictions off the book's analysis. 'Marx-type' industrial unrest is clearly predicted in the book, not least in China's great capitalist leap forward, which is tipped at several points as potentially producing 'autoworker labour unrest high points of world-historical significance' (p.95). But on the likelihood of a new labour-friendly international regime, an equivalent of the post-1945 social pacts in Europe and North America, emerging as the result of co-ordinated Polanyi-type resistance to neo-liberal globalization, Silver is much more cautious, inviting us to wait and see. Her final word, however, is a clarion call, 'Thus the ultimate challenge faced by the workers of the world in the early twenty-first century is the struggle, not just against one's own exploitation and exclusion, but for an international regime that truly subordinates profits to the livelihood of all.' This general challenge will be shared by any historian who is also a socialist. In this book Silver, though, has also issued a general challenge to labour historians to test her analytical approach and its key aspects. Many socialist historians will be content to rest with Silver's narrative mode of causal analysis, and with Polanyi's general insights into cycles of resistance to market forces. Marxist historians, though, will want to consider her theoretical framework and demonstrate how far value theory, not least unequal exchange theory, might provide a fuller explanation of the inter-relatedness of patterns of labour unrest she describes and on whose centrality she repeatedly insists.

Steve Ludlam
University of Sheffield

Martin van Gelderen and Quentin Skinner (eds), *Republicanism. A Shared European Heritage* (Cambridge University Press, Cambridge, 2002), vol.1, ISBN 0–521–80203–2, xi+420pp. and vol.2, ISBN 0–521–80756–5, xi+402pp., £45.00 each.

These two volumes constitute an unrivalled, comprehensive and supremely scholarly exploration of European republican thinking between the Renaissance and the Enlightenment. The editors and contributors are to be congratulated on the quality and ambition of the finished product.

Some readers of *Socialist History* may nonetheless wonder what such a collection—however impressive—can say to them. Surely, a few may think, the subject and period mean it must be largely irrelevant to historians concerned with studying class conflict and those individuals and institutions that attempted to advance the interests of the working class. If so, such readers need to be reminded that it was two decades ago that Gareth Stedman Jones in *Languages of Class* first underlined the importance of constitutional—as opposed to economic—issues to mid-nineteenth century Chartists. Against the conventional wisdom of the time, Stedman Jones questioned how far Chartism could be thought a specifically class-conscious, socialist movement. This was because he believed its adherents were mostly concerned with the individual's relationship to political authority, something broached by Parliamentary radicals before industrialisation had made much of an impact. In making his case for the importance of ideas that owed nothing to class sentiment to those normally viewed as quintessential working-class radicals, Stedman Jones only pointed back to the eighteenth century, but on the basis of this collection he should have gone further into the past.

Stedman Jones's essay was among the first (and certainly the most notable) instances of a once-Marxist historian taking the 'linguistic turn' by abandoning an exclusive (or in some cases even partial) reliance on materialism as the way to explain political developments. One does not however have to be a devotee of Saussurre or Foucault to believe that many ideas defined as socialist and embraced by what some still call the labour movement originated well before the industrial proletariat. For since Stedman Jones, among others, Miles Taylor has stressed the significance of constitutional issues to post-Chartist radicalism while Logie Barrow and Ian Bullock have written about the importance of such matters to ILP, SDF and Labour activists prior to 1914. Indeed, work by this reviewer and others on the post-1939 period shows how far Labour leaders anticipated the emergence of a kind of citizenship that owed little to what many still term Labourism and more to pre-industrial political thinking.

With that in mind, this collection provides much food for thought for social-ist historians willing to relax some of the seemingly impermeable barriers of period, subject and approach that mark off their interests from those of other historians. Some of the essays will obviously be of more interest than others. Moreover, we need to be aware—this is, after all, a collection co-edited by Quentin Skinner—that readers should avoid tracing simplistic lines of conti-nuity between thinking in the early modern period and that articulated in later contexts. Even so, it is apparent that republicans of the early modern period engaged with problems in very 'modern' ways indeed. For example, the essay by David Armitage reveals how some republican thinkers questioned how far the pursuit of liberty at home could be reconciled with the rise of overseas empires. Marco Geuna and David Winch furthermore remind us that even Adam Smith, a doyen of eighteenth-century republican thought, was oftentimes ambiguous about nascent commercial society—while others were so hostile Karl Marx cited their work to bolster his own arguments. More broadly, and maybe more contentiously, it is possible that republican concerns regarding the dangers of an overbearing state, outlined in numerous chapters, informed neo-revisionist social democratic responses to the post-war welfare state. As we know, such concerns now underpin thinking in many contemporary centre-left parties across Europe, most notably 'New' Labour. An appreciation of the European republican tradition, with its emphasis on positive as much as neg-ative liberty, should make us more sceptical that everything said by the likes of Tony Blair must be viewed a craven response to the dictates of Thatcherism. Progressive thinkers have long had good and honourable reasons to question how much power the state should exert.

There are now surely few historians—of socialism or any other subject—who do not consider that ideas, to a greater or lesser extent, construct understandings of what we take to be 'reality'. One does not need to be a post-modernist to believe that. Thus, everybody should now be concerned to understand the forms assumed by socialist thought and how these artic-ulated the actions of those bodies and individuals who believed they were advancing the popular interest. Similarly, few can not now believe that such ideas sprang directly out of social and economic actuality. Hence we all need to better appreciate the character of those intellectual systems that predated the development of capitalism so as to more properly comprehend the char-acter of socialism. Indeed, collections such as *Republicanism* raise questions about the extent to which socialism marked the kind of radical epistemo-logical break once confidently assumed by partisans of the left.

Steven Fielding
Salford University

Steven Fielding, *The Labour Governments 1964–1970*, vol.1. *Labour and Cultural Change* (Manchester University Press, Manchester, 2003), ISBN 0–7190–4364–6, 259pp., £45.00.

This study of the Labour Party's internal developments during the period of Wilson's 1964 landslide victory and subsequent surprising electoral defeat in 1970 is the first of a three-volume series investigating different aspects of the government's record. Benefiting from recently released government files, it highlights explanations for the relative lack of achievement both in the country and inside the Labour Party itself during the 1960s. Some of the factors identified included the party nature and leadership; and the delicate state of the British economy, declining in the world order, with the population blighted by a growing individualism.

Fielding's readable contribution to Labour Party analysis provides an enjoyable glimpse into the schizophrenic 1960s of post-modern revolt restrained by undercurrents of tired conformism. The book addresses culturally important issues around the emerging 'equalities' agenda by dedicating a chapter to submerged issues of class, gender, age and race, in terms of the party's long-term electoral, ideological and organisational problems, mirrored by its lacklustre performance whilst briefly in government. Developing a cultural revisionist approach chronologically into the 1960s, the text focuses on social change within a cultural history of politics. Embracing post-modern contributions which have thus far problematised the direct nature of the party's relationship with people, Fielding interrogates this with regard to Labour's attitudes towards workers, women, immigrants and the young, including insights from seven regional; four borough and forty constituency labour parties in an attempt to include the views of the party's most humble active members, combining to offer a 'total history' of the Labour Party of the period.

In exploring each aspect of equality policy Fielding revealed a growing awareness among voters and political activists of social inclusion agendas, undoubtedly reinforced by the fact that each of these constituencies would be natural Labour voters, and hopefully reward the party of government for equality reforms in their favour. However, somehow neither the reforms nor the reward ever bore fruit.

Overall his discussion of the Labour Party hinges on the underpinning schism in the party around modernisation and equality, consolidated by the final chapter charting the party's failure to institutionalise its youth movement, despite introducing legislation lowering the voting age to 18 for the 1970 election, yet which Labour still lost spectacularly. Emphasis is placed on modernity throughout the thesis: in relation to equalising women's pay and role within marriage; social integration of black immigrants; keeping up to date with changes to the manufacturing industry's working classes; and the changing demands of the nation's youth. Modernity challenged organisational, structural and ideological traditions within the party which, as Fielding pointed out, had not reformed its antiquated internal structures and party organisational methods since 1918, despite the radical context particularly of the post-war period. Essentially, all the talk of reform on the left came to naught, both internally to Labour and externally in its government record. Nonetheless, Fielding indicates that the talking itself may prove to be an important consultation phase in discussing and revising the party's policy. Indeed he ties many of the party's debates to intellectual pamphlets such as those distributed by the Fabian Society (such as Crosland's *Future of Socialism*), as well as to Governmental white papers, perpetuating the debate across the country. Hence one implication of this mid-1960s reform discourse is that although the book focused its analysis on measurable outputs of policy implementation, much of the evidence put forward supports the suggestion that if Wilson's leadership engaged the party in wide-reaching debates on widening access to representation, and his government launched public debates on equality, then this achievement—however undervalued by the electorate—was in itself an important task, laying the foundations for concrete reform in the future.

In this sense the study offers new empirical evidence for the historical context behind later reforms. This important text draws neatly together research agendas on popular culture, party organisation, political participation and democratic accountability in a social historical analysis. Beyond the research market, this could offer a core reader for undergraduate courses on social change in the modern British political system.

Julia Speht
University of Wolverhampton

John Keane, *Global Civil Society?* (Cambridge University Press, Cambridge, 2003), ISBN 0–521–89462–X, 234pp., £14.99 pbk.

If there is one term, one idea, that has achieved more currency than any other since the collapse of the Soviet-style communist states at the end of the1980s it is that of *civil society*. It is as though an idea, coined in the eighteenth century, had languished in the intellectual doldrums until the time was right for its full potential to be realised. That time, it turned out, happened to be the moment when free-market capitalism seemed to triumph over its most important ideological rival—communism. Certainly, those right-wing intellectuals who rushed to the newly liberated former-communist states to preach the virtues of the free market found, in the idea of civil society, a useful societal motif with which to balance the drier economic prescriptions they carried with them. Absent from its great ideological rival, free-market capitalism seemed finally to have gone global, taking, it seemed, the idea of civil society with it.

The problem with this scenario is that by *fiat* it restricts both the content and the scope of the term *civil society* to a narrow range of ideas and applications. For example, yoking the idea of civil society to the 'triumph' of a particular version of capitalism may lead us to question the relevance of the idea to, or even the existence of, the thing named, in those contexts which do not share the requisite characteristics. Where free-market capitalism is rejected, as it is, for example, by some Islamic states, there can, by definition, be no civil society. The danger here is that *civil society* becomes just another ideological stick with which the Western capitalist hegemony can beat the rest of the world. Civil society is *civilized* society, and the non-Westernised, non-capitalist societies are therefore not civilized. It is colonialism, by another name.

In a series of thoughtful and provocative books and articles John Keane has worked diligently to understand and articulate a plausible concept of civil society—one that both reflects the diversity of civil societies in the world, and as free as possible from the destructive ideological baggage of both the right (e.g. free-market dogmatists and ideologues) and the left (e.g. Gramsci-inspired theorists—such as Hardt and Negri—who see civil society as a potentially autonomous entity standing over against the state and its capitalist shell). These 'purists' of right and left, it is claimed, oversimplify the intense complexity of the relationship between state, economy, and the vast array of civil society associations working at the macro, meso and micro-levels, within, between, across and beyond state boundaries.

Keane's project here is to chart this complexity, not only in terms of the vast array of groups and associations that unite individuals in civil association, but also in terms of the multiplicity of levels—'local, national, regional, and supranational'—at which this 'vast mosaic of socio-economic groups, organisations and initiatives' (p.129) may operate. Underpinning this project is a desire on Keane's part to establish—against those who would deny such a thing—the important role still played by *political* institutions whether in the form of local government, the state, or multinational entities such as the European Union, both in regulating the environment in which such groups operate, and in responding to the diligent work performed by such crucial civil society organisations as NGOs. Rather than a simplistic opposition between civil society associations and such political institutions—the classic, and still important, idea of civil society as scrutineer—Keane sees such associations performing a variety of important supportive roles too. Such organisations are flexible and innovative where states cannot be, and can work to alert states and other political bodies to potential risks and disasters.

Rooting discussions of civil society within the traditional political entity of the state, as the classic account of civil society did, ignores both the way in which some civil society associations and movements transgress state boundaries, and the fact of an increasingly global 'framework of governance in which both States and civil society associations play a part. civil society is, Keane argues, over-determined by various forces (economic, political, social, cultural) and it is a mistake to think that states, either as direct actors or as signatories to multinational agreements, do not play a significant part in sustaining and regulating civil society, even on a global scale. But it is also the case that in the emerging demands of civil society associations lies real potential for making this global system more accountable.

If Keane is concerned to insist upon keeping politics in the picture, as some civil society theorists are not, then he is also concerned to keep economics in the picture too. Keane is aware of the wealth-creating potential of capitalism and does not see global civil society as 'something like a world proletariat in civvies' (p.65) destined to overthrow it. He is aware of the importance, however cynical, of capitalist corporations as sources of funding for NGOs, for example, just as he is aware that the demands for social justice made by some civil society associations are targeted at these corporations. But he is also aware that civil associations of various sorts exist in non-capitalist countries too, so that it is a mistake to associate civil society solely with free market capitalism.

The book, reflecting the object(s) it seeks to describe, is rich with examples of civil society associations drawn from across the globe. Indeed, if there is one drawback with the book it lies in the sense one gets of seeing far more trees than wood. It is as though we can see examples of civil society everywhere, but are never told flat-out—normatively-speaking—what it is. We are, of course, familiar with the idea that civil society is usually characterised in terms of concepts such as tolerance, civility, reasonableness, accountability, democracy, liberty, perhaps even social justice. It may even be characterised in terms of human rights, which may be said to embody many of these concepts. But all of these concepts are controversial and are themselves objects of struggle.

These issues are addressed in the concluding chapter—'Ethics Beyond

Borders.' Here Keane engages with a series of debates which look at the question of whether or not there can be an adequate ethical underpinning uniting the diverse moralities—religious or secular—that a global civil society necessarily must accommodate. To cut a long—but not uninteresting—story short, Keane believes that admission to global civil society calls for adherence on the part of these diverse moralities to a 'non-foundationist' ethic which is basically characterised by an acceptance of plurality. Hence the great enemy of global civil society is assertive monism of whatever stripe this might be. As Keane puts it: 'Monism is always and everywhere a threat to the pluralism of civil society,' and although it does not follow that all forms of monism are necessarily a clear and present threat, nevertheless 'the friends of global civil society must always keep an open mind about the different forms of monism that spring up within its spaces, or threaten it from outside.' (p.203)

The problem here, of course, lies in the phrase 'the friends of global civil society', for this tends to reify the concept of global civil society which elsewhere, and as the many examples catalogued here show, names a contingent outcome of a wide range of diverse activities. The 'friends' of global civil society are not friends of that concept at all; they are friends rather of the many and varied causes and concerns they pursue at their macro, meso, and micro-levels of operation. It is not at all clear therefore who, if anyone, is to police the monists. At the moment, if those monists come to plant bombs in our shopping malls or fly aeroplanes into the walls of our cities, it is not the combined forces of global civil society that galvanises against them, it is the self-styled defender of civilisation and the New World Order the hegemonic United States of America.

These concerns aside, Keane is well aware of the fragility of global civil society—the question mark in the title is testament to this—yet the tone of the book overall is cautiously optimistic. Keane is a well-travelled and sure-footed guide to this complex subject, but he is also a guide who is aware of the many pitfalls that the building of a global civil society might encounter. In such difficult and complex terrain, Keane is the best sort of guide to have.

Alan Apperley
University of Wolverhampton

Lawrence Black, *The Political Culture of the Left in Affluent Britain, 1951–64. Old Labour, New Britain?* (Macmillan, Basingstoke, 2003), ISBN 0–333–96836–0, ix+263pp., £45.00 hbk.

Lawrence Black's book examines socialists' uneasiness with the growing consumerism and mass commercial culture that was felt to have sustained the Conservative Party in office during the 'Thirteen Wasted Years'. The book divides into three sections, each of two chapters. The first section discusses the culture and character of the left itself, for example its moralism, belief in the need for citizens' active participation, and view of emotions as evidence of weakness. The second looks at its interpretation of the social changes associated with affluence, such as 'Americanization', and the growth of suburbia (socialists were at ease in either country or town, but not in the suburban straddling of the two). In general, as with its hostility to hire-purchase, commercial television, and advertising, the left's feelings towards the acquisitiveness and triviality of affluence were negative. The third assesses the left's attempts then to respond on the basis of its interpretation, and highlights both the limited responses of the majority, and the more active attempt of the minority, including revisionists, especially Crosland, and 'modernizers' to adapt Labour to meet the above changes. The enthusiasm of Tony Benn for using new communication techniques, and his masterminding of the party's 1959 election broadcasts, are noted as features 'that would have his latter-day persona (more conscious of socialist tradition) wincing' (p.179). But the dominant picture painted by Black is of a movement 'disinclined to change with the times' and suffering in popularity for it (p.187).

This very good book, with an economical writing style, is a welcome contribution to the growing body of work on the cultural dimension of the left, and will complement works on earlier and later periods, including Chris Waters's *British Socialists and the Politics of Popular Culture, 1884–1914* (Manchester, 1990) and Steven Fielding's *The Labour Governments 1964–70: volume 1: Labour and cultural change* (Manchester, 2003). It has three main strengths. First, through its wealth of detail, especially from grassroots Labour sources, the book is distinctive in the extent to which it portrays the 'totality' of the left. It combines study of national leadership and grassroots; party and people; communist, New Left, and Labour; determinism and agency (broad social trends, but also the left's power to shape its own destiny); and policy, organisation, behaviour, and attitudes. This opens up discussion of a range of different connections across spheres of left history often kept separate. So, for example, socialist suspicion at the urbanity or philandering of revisionists is highlighted as much as opposition to their policies (pp.28, 35). The multi-faceted strands within the party are emphasised. Thus, divisions are explored between puritans and pluralists, and also (a further and separate divide) those who sought in the materially affluent 1950s to give a new emphasis to non-material cultural issues and those, such as Harold Wilson, who came to place a renewed stress on economic priorities.

Second, the book feeds into some important developing historiographical and political science schools. As noted above, it belongs to the school of interest in left political culture, which examines 'informal, instinctive and ethical impulses' as much as 'more formal or explicitly ideological reasoning' (p.2). Such a focus usefully complicates traditional narratives of Labour Party history built around the divide between left and right factions within the party. Gaitskell and Bevan alike dismissed new domestic goods as 'gadgets' (pp.27–8). It also draws on the 'new political history', which sees politics and political parties as having agencies of their own, not simply determined by economic and social forces, so that the apparent erosion of Labour's traditional support base in this period was not bound to be damaging, had the party responded to affluence in more positive and imaginative ways. And it adds to the historiography on the moral dimension of socialism, drawing for example on Black's earlier work on the Socialist Union, which demanded that its members practise their socialism in their personal lives. It cites Peggy Crane pondering whether a Labour member who had stopped attending ward meetings to work instead on a school care committee 'was not a better socialist than many of us who spend two or three evenings a week on party business', and notes Fred Mulley's declaration that 'example is still better than precept' (pp.32–3). Finally, the book echoes the revisionist work of Steven Fielding and others in emphasising the limits to the popular appeal of socialism, 'even amongst Labour voters', the sense of socialists as 'an earnest rather than representative sample of the working class' (pp.7, 189).

Third, we are provided with a consistent picture of a socialist culture which was 'complacent, conservative, almost old-fashioned' (p.10), despite this being a period when the Labour Party as an institution was in some ways at the height of its strength and social importance. This was not inevitable. Socialists are seen as having 'brought about much of their alienation from popular affluence' (p.122). Affluence, whether home ownership or rock 'n'roll, did not have an innate political meaning hostile to the left. Thus, had they responded in more nuanced ways, they could have both preserved some of their principles *and* responded more positively to affluence, and thus retained popularity. For example, in discussing socialist attitudes to television and advertising, Black notes that 'much of the left saw its struggles as *against* these new media rather than *within* debates about their uses' (p.187).

The book lacks balance in one important area. In focusing on the damage that unqualified condemnation of affluence caused Labour, it is, in common with most other books in the growing historiography of Labour's political culture, too critical of that strand on the left which sought morally and intellectually to improve people. To assert that socialists' 'very prescriptive attitudes, moralism and reliance on the state as an improving agent' were 'at the root of their unpopularity' (p.9) or that 'the frequently moralistic rhetoric of branch activists and the left generally could contribute deleteriously to perceptions of socialism' (p.192) is to over-simplify. The part of socialism, drawing on Victorian liberalism which sought to uplift morally, educate, and culturally improve the citizenry, whether through personal example, by viewing comprehensive schools as a vehicle for spreading academic excellence, or by supporting the BBC's Third Programme, was indispensable if the ideology was ultimately to succeed. After all, a socialist society required citizens who were not just materially secure, but altruistic and rational. Black is correct that there was a problem, both intrinsically and electorally with too much *moralising*. But the hedonistic excesses, greed, and low quality of much popular leisure and culture in British society forty years on from the book's period suggest there was at least as much of a problem of too little *morality*. Black implies that socialists' late-1950s' assumption that 'the people themselves, besides much in popular culture, were barriers to socialist progress' was misguided, and that their appearance as 'an élite, moral vanguard' was damaging (pp. 8–9). In fact, people and popular culture *were* such a barrier, and Labour was correct to maintain a moral and intellectual vanguard tradition, as New Labour has done with its revival of the traditional socialist belief in responsibility, fiscal probity, and intellectual improvement through free museum entry and high standards in schools.

But this succinct book will well repay those reading it, and should be of interest to those drawn to political, cultural, or social history alike.

Jeremy Nuttall
Queens University, Belfast

Catherine Epstein, *The Last Revolutionaries: German Communists and Their Century* (Harvard University Press, Cambridge, MA and London, 2003), ISBN 0–674–01045–0, xi+322pp., $29.95 hbk.

This book is an ambitious study of a generation of veteran communists who were born in Germany in the pre-1914 era, joined the communist party

(KPD) prior to Hitler's seizure of power in 1933, and who lived through tumultuous times, enduring terrible privations and persecution, but also enjoying their post-1945 status as the 'victors of History' in the German Democratic Republic. For those individuals who survived into old age in the 1990s, they also experienced the pain of belonging, once again, to a 'scorned political movement' (p.1); this generation, now largely dead or dying, ended its days vanquished by History.

Epstein sets herself the task of writing a collective biography of this veteran communist generation, described imaginatively by Anne McElvoy as the 'unimprovables'.[1] The author explicitly focuses upon the lived experience of a small number of leading individuals, rather than providing detailed scrutiny of the developing KPD/SED ideology, or the organisational character of the movement. Although these aspects of German communist history are considered tangentially by Epstein, they are analysed within the context of a clear focus on veteran communists (from the leading organs of the party), and their particular influence upon the trajectory of the movement. She claims that 'the collective biography of veteran communists is paradigmatic of the twentieth-century communist experience', and that the 'defining attribute' of these individuals was their 'fervent loyalty to the party and its cause.' (p.3)

The book's narrative is organised chronologically, and interweaves the life-stories of eight veteran communists (Franz Dahlem, Gerhart Eisler, Erich Honecker, Emmy Koenen, Fred Oelßner, Karl Schirdewan, Fritz Selbmann and Walter Ulbricht), five of whom were members, at various times, of the Politburo and all eight of the Central Committee/Party Executive. These individuals were all dedicated and unswerving in their communist conviction, and Epstein argues that they were representative, at least to this extent, of the 60,000-strong cohort of veteran communists that played a disproportionate role in the life of the SED and the GDR, enjoyed 'tremendous authority and prestige', and became 'the voice of the regime's official memory' (p.2). The unswerving nature of their Stalinist ideological commitment, in the face of the dissolution of the KPD, imprisonment, purges and bewildering changes of party line, is truly remarkable. Epstein points out that very few members of this political generation ended up as dissidents or 'reformers', but she does concede that her definition of such activity is 'rather strict' (p.8). Still, it is remarkable that 'virtually all' members of this generation remained constant in their belief that 'communist power once attained should not be attenuated, much less relinquished' (p.9). Very few members of this political generation renounced their communist identity, even in the face of dramatic fluctuations in their personal fortunes within the movement.

However, despite their common experience as high-ranking members of the SED, this cohort nonetheless followed diverse life paths, perhaps most significantly in the period 1933–1949. Some spent these years in exile in the Soviet Union; others in exile in the liberal democratic West (often in France, but also in the USA or Mexico); others spent at least part of this period fighting Franco's fascism in Spain with the International Brigades; finally, others remained in Nazi Germany and took part in the resistance movement (many spending long periods incarcerated in the concentration camps). Epstein argues convincingly that these different experiences did not necessarily lead to the adoption of identifiably divergent positions in the GDR. She rejects the idea that veteran communists who survived the Nazi camps (e.g. Schirdewan, Selbmann and Dahlem), or were exposed to Western, liberal democratic ideas (e.g. Eisler) 'advocated a more tolerant or humane form of socialism' (pp.8, 71–83), just as she argues that those who spent their exile in the Soviet Union (e.g. Oelßner) were not perceptibly more likely to espouse Stalinist ideological norms (pp.83–5). Indeed, if anything, her research suggests that those who survived in the camps did so, at least in part, *as a result* of their unquestioning 'adherence to party discipline', and this was more likely to make such individuals deeply antagonistic to would-be reformers in the SED/GDR. Similarly, those communists in exile in the West were often persecuted, harassed and imprisoned, and these experiences also confirmed them in their disdain for capitalist systems (pp.85–99).

Epstein summarises for the reader her understanding of the historical debate concerning 'the SED's legitimizing myth' (p.248) of antifascism in the GDR, a debate that has been particularly acute over the past decade. She discusses Lutz Niethammer's research on the role played by veteran communists in the concentration camp system, and appears to concur that communists 'had been complicit in upholding the brutal SS regime in Buchenwald' (p.249).[2] Discussing Selbmann and Schirdewan's incarceration in Sachsenhausen, and Dahlem's experiences at Mauthausen, Epstein points out that these years entailed 'a paradoxical tale of courage and complicity, solidarity and sordidness' (p.72). She seems to recognise that 'prison and camp conditions also precluded inner-party democracy', and that pre-1933 KPD cadres only survived precisely because they had practised a 'model solidarity toward each other' (p.82). Nevertheless, Epstein hints at her sympathy with Niethammer's stress upon the moral compromises engaged in by communist inmates, and concludes that the maintenance of 'their Stalinist political culture even in the face of Nazi inhumanity '[is] a chilling reminder of the human propensity to answer persecution with persecution' (p.79). The drastically changed character of the commemoration of the camps in the period since 1990 in the ex-GDR, which has shifted from an official discourse extolling the communist-led resistance movement to viewing these sites as sources of 'national shame' (as they have been understood in the FRG throughout the post-war era), is obviously of great historical and contemporary significance. This question arouses passionate and partisan debate; Epstein, in an interview with Hilde Eisler (Gerhart's widow) in 1995, was told in no uncertain terms that the 'decreed antifascism' of the GDR was infinitely preferable to the 'anti-antifascism' prevalent in the united Germany. For this reviewer, at least, the complexity and real dilemmas of the communist position in the concentration camps, and of the moral and political conditions faced by veteran German communists, is well expressed in Jorge Semprún's *Quel beau dimanche!* (1980):[3] 'One had to resist; that was the first point. In order to do so, one had to use every opportunity, however small, offered by the order imposed by the SS themselves; that was the second point. Therefore, the German Communists in Buchenwald were right, historically, to wrest scraps of power in the internal administration of the camp.' (p.151)

Epstein makes use of a broad range of sources, including poignant interviews with surviving veteran communists in the mid-1990s, when most of them were well into their eighties; they were, she suggests, 'brilliant evaders of questions' (p.251). Interestingly, she finds few useful documents in the archives of the *Stasi* specifically relating to this generation, speculating that its loyalty to the regime was so evident that surveillance was not believed to be necessary. Apart from the interviews, Epstein makes very good use of the SED party archives (now housed in the *Bundesarchiv* in Berlin). Perhaps the most original part of the book, however, is the methodological discussion concerning the manipulation of veteran communists' biographies. Epstein uses published autobiographical writings, as well as party personnel files, unpublished memoirs, correspondence and reminiscences, and she studies the role of the SED's Institute of Marxism-Leninism (Memoir Section of the Central Party Archive) in the production of the regime's 'official memory'. The importance of this 'administration of memory', to use Niethammer's phrase, to an understanding of the twists and turns of party policy, especially with regard to the purges of the 1950s (as well as the prospect for rehabilitation of those purged) is very clearly borne out by Epstein.

This book is a rich and rewarding one, with original, though occasionally contentious, insights in a number of fields. As a study of communist political commitment and identity, as expressed by a particular political generation, this work deserves to find a wide audience. Over a decade ago, in a review of another excellent book analysing similar themes to the present volume, I argued that the study of the collective biography of 'the Last True Communists' should become a new genre of communist historiography.[4] This work admirably shows the way for further study, and sets an impressive standard.

Stephen Hopkins
University of Leicester

Notes

1. Anne McElvoy, *The Saddled Cow: East Germany's Life and Legacy* (London, 1992), p.25.
2. Lutz Niethammer (ed.), *Der 'Gesäuberte' Antifaschismus: Die SED und die roten Kapos von Buchenwald* (Berlin, 1994).
3. Jorge Semprún, a leading communist in the 1950s and early 1960s, left the Spanish communist party in 1964. He was exiled from Spain after Franco's victory, fought with the French communist resistance, was arrested in 1943 and deported to Buchenwald. His meditation on this experience was published as *Quel beau dimanche!* (Paris, 1980). The quotation is taken from the English translation, *What a Beautiful Sunday!* (London, 1984). For a fuller treatment of this question, and Semprún's comparison of the Nazi camps with the Soviet gulag, see pp.143–62.
4. Jaff Schatz, *The Generation: The Rise and Fall of the Jewish Communists of Poland* (Berkeley, CA, 1991). See my review in *Journal of Communist Studies*, 8, no.3 (September 1992), pp.148–50.

Matthew Worley (ed.), *In Search of Revolution: International Communist Parties in the Third Period* (I B Tauris, London, 2004), ISBN 1–85043–407–7, 379pp., £45.00 hbk.

Officially proclaimed at the Comintern's sixth world congress in 1928, the so-called Third Period of 'post-war capitalism' was based on the conviction that capitalist stabilisation was not only not becoming any stronger, but, on the contrary, was becoming 'increasingly undermined'. 'Gigantic class battles' were supposed to result from these new 'contradictions of world capitalism' and, in this context, the national sections of the Comintern had the task of leading the workers under the banner of 'class against class'. In a very stimulating introductory essay, the editor of this new collection of essays claims: 'More often than not, historical references to the theories and policies of the Third Period are closely followed by a variation on the term disaster'. No other period in the Comintern's history has had as bad a reputation as this one. Trotsky called it the 'Third Period of Comintern error' and the majority of communist parties lost membership and influence during this time. For many, if not most historians, the sectarian tendency of this period, along with the recurring condemnation of social democracy as 'social fascism', weakened the left by sharpening hostilities between the communists and the majority of organised and politically conscious workers. One consequence, the most calamitous of all, was to make possible the rise to power of fascism in Germany. This turn to the left was not imposed without significant resistance; for example in Italy, where Umberto Terracini and Antonio Gramsci showed their opposition. Many communists, particularly in France, welcomed the ending of the Third Period in 1934–5, and the adoption of the popular front policy at the Comintern's seventh and last world congress in July–August 1935.

The strength of this book is that it clearly shows that the 1928 'turn to the left' was welcomed by many communists, especially in the ranks of the unemployed, semi-skilled and unskilled workers, and in the ranks of the new generation of communist leaders, frustrated by tainted politics and failures from previous years. The experiment of the Anglo-Russian Trade Union Committee and the subordination of the Chinese Communist Party to the Guomindang nationalist policy not only led to dramatic failures for the working class—such as Chiang Kai-shek's repression of the labour movement in Shanghai—but corrupted the very idea of communist parties as an autonomous political force.

The very wide range of communist parties considered in this collection — German, British, Italian, French, Yugoslavian, Latvian, Portuguese, Spanish, American, Canadian, Australian, New Zealand, Chinese, Indian, South African and Brazilian—gives a good idea of the reception of the new policy in different national contexts. Some Comintern sections, such as the German CP, examined here by Norman LaPorte, played a central role in the introduction of the theory of 'social fascism'. More than any order from Moscow, the shooting of German May Day marchers on the orders of the SPD police chief Zörgiebel in 1929 helped convince German communists that this notion was appropriate. In Spain, writes Tim Rees, it was during this time that the PCE became for the first time an organised and disciplined party, and the 'class against class' line was abandoned only reluctantly, and with many adverse consequences. According to John Manley's contribution, the adoption of the Third Period line in Canada was also rooted in national conditions, while in New Zealand, according to Kerry Taylor, the explanation for the 1928 'left turn' and the ongoing influence of sectarianism after 1935, lies more in the contours of the national political scene than in the corridors of the Comintern.

Changes in the social composition of the communist movement are another important key to understanding the Third Period. By 1935, unemployed members constituted 52 per cent of the total membership of the American CP. In Britain, as communist influence among organised workers diminished, communist activity among the unemployed increased and the CP headed the pre-eminent unemployed organisation of the time, the National Unemployed Workers' Movement. Even in Britain, communist party membership consequently recovered from the low point reached in 1930. In Germany, the KPD reached its membership peak when it spoke the language of 'social fascism'.

The Third Period thus needed to be reinvestigated in order to reach beyond oversimplified interpretations. First, the New Line had some roots in earlier periods—ultra-leftist tactics had been in evidence in 1924–5 in the German and the Latvian parties—and some aspects of the Fourth Period already existed during the Third. Furthermore, both theories and strategies of the Third Period passed through a number of different phases—four, according to Matthew Worley. As Geoffrey Swain explains in the conclusion of his interesting comparison of the Latvian and Yugoslavian communist parties, the 'speed with which individual parties responded to this evolution in the Comintern line depended on the political views of individual Communist leaders'. Finally, historians often forget that the crisis of the 1930s was a bad period not only for the Comintern but for the labour movement in general. As Patricia Stranahan notes in connection with China, though communist leaders in Moscow initiated policies that were doomed from the outset, it was also a period when economic, social and political conditions were so unfavourable that even the best-led revolutionary movement would have had a difficult time succeeding.

With this in mind, the Comintern's new policy must be approached in relation to factors other than the crisis of capitalism, or the assault launched by the Stalinist leadership against the left, and subsequently, right oppositions within the Soviet party. Changes in the international diplomatic scene are one important consideration. In the book's second introductory essay dedicated to the Comintern's colonial policy, John Callaghan is right to recall how weak the international position of the Soviet Union was at the time. Many European countries, as well as the Americas and Eastern countries, still withheld diplomatic recognition. The broken relations with Britain; the worsening of relations with France and China; the new westerly direction taken by German foreign policy, in joining the League of Nations and signing the Young Plan—all this convinced the Soviets that the central global contradiction was no longer inside the imperialist camp, but ran between the imperialist front of capitalist countries and the USSR, supported of course by the revolutionary workers of those capitalist countries. From this moment on, the unconditional defence of the USSR became the driving force behind the whole international strategy of the Soviets.

Already this was symbolised by the first Friends of the Soviet Union Congress, a sort of new Soviet International, which took place in 1927 in the wake of the celebrations commemorating the tenth anniversary of the October Revolution. The 'Class Against Class' line taken up from the Comintern's sixth congress the following summer should therefore also be seen as a means of strengthening the dependency (or subordination) of national communist parties in relation to Moscow. This especially comes to light through the choice of executives like Walter Ulbricht, Stewart Smith, Sam Carr and Heitor Ferreira Lima. All were trained at the International Lenin School in Moscow, and all enjoyed little national credibility, but were prepared for spectacular political changes (such as *de facto* support of the 1939–41 alliance with the Nazis) in the interest of the USSR alone.

The threat to the 'workers' fatherland' which served as justification for Russia's Third Revolution (the drive to socialism) was too good a weapon not to make use of in the destruction of Stalin's opponents. The Third Period must in this sense also be linked to Stalin's fight against the right wing and so-called conciliatory elements, even though Bukharin as their most prominent representative was one of the first to have spoken about the emergence of a 'third period of historical development'. In this way the turn to the left was used by Stalin to 'internationalise' the fight against Bukharin and his followers, with the help of an ambitious young prole-tarian generation of communist leaders, including Ulbricht, Maurice Thorez and Josip Tito. This official new leftist line was also very useful in reducing the room for manoeuvre of the Trotskyist opposition, then exiled in Siberia, whose leftist criticism of both Moscow and Comintern policy needed to be deflected by the Soviet leadership. Though Trotsky did not originally oppose Chinese communists entering the Guomindang, from April 1926 he argued that the communists should leave the Nationalist party. So when the Shanghai communists were massacred on 12 April 1927, the policy of the Comintern in China became one of the favourite targets of the left opposition. Given this, it is not surprising that during the sixth world congress the 'formation of any kind of block between the com-munist party and the national-reformist opposition' was rejected. This sectarian policy had bad effects on front organisations such as the League Against Imperialism. The imported categories of the new line that had been constructed in the context of power struggles in the Soviet Union and

Europe were not directly applicable to early 1930s' South African or Indian conditions. Consequently, as Allison Drew explains, they had little if any resonance with local politics. In the colonial world, the communist parties, when they existed at all, were still small sects, such as in India. Not all the contributions to this collection manage to link the story of national Comintern sections with these Soviet and international factors. Nevertheless, it is one of the merits of the books to show that the ultra-left line was not so monolithic as is often argued. It needs to be thought of in terms of the interaction of different levels, from local to international, even if the main impulse came from Moscow.

This Comintern's Third Period therefore reveals itself as the fundamental driving force which would 'ensure independence and absolute otherness' of the communist parties in relation to their national context and political system, with a distinct communist culture, specific values and iron discipline. One of the appeals of this book, whose other contributors are Aldo Agosti, Carlos Cunha, Stephen Hopkins, Stuart Macintyre, James Ryan and Marco Santana, is that it allows us to follow the process through various national sections' history, some of which are very little known. And if we want to keep in mind something positive about the period, why not remember that the Comintern paid particular attention to the issue of race? After all, it was at this time—more than two decades before the modern American civil rights movement—that communists in countries like Australia and the USA began seriously to combat racism within and outside their own organisations.

Jean-François Fayet
University of Geneva